DOWN THE YELLOW BRICK ROAD

DOWN THE YELLOW BRICK ROAD

The Making of The Wizard of Oz

By Doug McClelland

Bonanza Books
New York

This 1989 edition is published by Bonanza Books,
distributed by Crown Publishers, Inc., 225 Park Avenue
South, New York, New York 10003, by arrangement with
Ottenheimer Publishers, Inc.

Printed in the United States of America

Library of Congress Cataloging-in-Publication Data

McClelland, Doug.
    Down the yellow brick road : the making of the
  Wizard of Oz / by Doug McClelland.
      p.   cm.
    ISBN 0-517-69911-7
    1. Wizard of Oz (Motion picture)   I. Title
PN1997.W593M34   1989
791.43'72 – dc20   89-38778
                                                   CIP

h g f e d c b

*This book is dedicated to all
my nieces and nephews, in the
order of their appearance:*

JIMMY

EDDIE

KIM

MARK

BONNIE

SHERRI

JIMMY

WAYNE

ERIC

JEANNE

The Wizard of Oz
of
by L. Frank Baum

ACKNOWLEDGMENTS

Much gratitude for their help to Irene Burns; CBS Archives; Cinemabilia; George Cukor; Buddy Ebsen; David Finkle; Margaret Hamilton; Miles Kreuger; Larry Edmunds Bookshop; Kenneth G. Lawrence, Movie Memorabilia Shop; Leonard Maltin; NBC-TV, New York; Movie Star News; the Museum of Modern Art Film Archives; James Robert Parish; Mike Sigman, *Record World;* Theatre Collection and Staff, New York Public Library for the Performing Arts; Richard Thorpe; Jerry Vermilye; Walter Wager, ASCAP; and my editor, Ted Sennett.

Special thanks to Lou Valentino, a wizard at helping me locate rare photographs.

The most thanks, however, to Metro-Goldwyn-Mayer for the creation of the film masterpiece, *The Wizard of Oz.*

Doug McClelland
Bradley Beach, N.J.

CONTENTS

The Picture 1

"... and to the young in heart we dedicate this picture ..."

*T*he Metro-Goldwyn-Mayer Studio included that line in the written foreword to *The Wizard of Oz*, a bit nervous, perhaps, at the launching of their costly production. For one thing, the year 1939, with its darkening clouds, hardly seemed a propitious time for fairy tales or fantasy. In addition, the L. Frank Baum story had been filmed before, unsuccessfully, and Paramount's not dissimilar *Alice in Wonderland* had been a flop earlier in the decade.

As Auntie Em might have said, "Pish-tosh." MGM's movie was an instant hit; and, afterward, thanks to annual prime time television showings, more people have seen it than any other motion picture ever made. It seems safe to say that *The Wizard of Oz* has charmed plenty of the *old* in heart, too. For once, the public's taste is unimpugned: there is not a scene—indeed, hardly a moment—in this ambitious undertaking that doesn't sing with life and love and the kind of imagination and craftsmanship Hollywood could muster during its Golden Age.

There are so many reasons (and not all are visible) for the spell this celluloid cornucopia has cast over generations that only a book can begin to detail them. The most obvious is the presence of the tragic wren known as Judy Garland, then a bright-eyed, rosy-cheeked, pudgy teen-ager portraying Dorothy, the wistful little prairie flower created by Baum in his venerated book and its sequels. On the threshold of one of the entertainment world's legendary careers, the horrors of self-abuse and exploitation yet to come, Judy was clearly a natural. She knew how to get a laugh, how to get a tear. She knew how to make unforgettably poignant a light, unscarred but sensitive barnyard rendition of "Over the Rainbow." Several lifetimes later, she would dangle too-slim legs into stuffy concert hall pits and give a ravaged, soul-surging interpretation of this song, now her signature number, that would evoke a torrent of love from audiences who—helped by the inevitable *The Wizard of Oz*—remembered when.

Not that Dorothy was any Scarlett O'Hara in histrionic (or musical) opportunities. Judy wasn't even starred; on screen she got merely "with" billing in the same modest lettering as her co-players, although she was listed first. It was an endearing role, endearingly performed, but it did not plumb the depths of Judy's talent. (Too few of her films did.) She was, in fact, at sixteen a shade too mature even for the "well-grown child for her age" described by Frank Baum and originally slated for the younger Shirley Temple, whose studio, 20th Century-Fox, made her unavailable. MGM

13

flattened out Judy's bustline, groomed her in blue pinafores, anklets and red-tinted pigtails and, abetted by their diminutive actress, pulled it off.

Some of the other roles were much more colorful than Judy's; plenty of scene-stealing went on. Several of the parts were dual in nature: Ray Bolger as the Scarecrow, Jack Haley as the Tin Woodman, Bert Lahr as the Cowardly Lion and Margaret Hamilton as the Wicked Witch of the West all had progenitors in Dorothy's real life away from the dream Land of Oz. As did Wizard Frank Morgan, who played a half-dozen different characters. (His versatility in the film is too often slighted.) Each of these seasoned troupers appeared inspired, as did the rest.

The mammoth Mervyn LeRoy production itself was dazzling, a splash of one-time-only cinema art stunningly guided by (mostly) director Victor Fleming. A masterstroke was the decision to shoot MGM's somewhat expressionistic, bleak, flat Kansas land in Sepia—thus suggesting the parched environment as well as fine beige paper-stock—and the storybook swirls of the never-never Land of Oz in brilliant Technicolor. (Viewing it today on television, where muddy color is the modern rule, the vivid, primary hues of this middle-aged movie fairly leap from the box.) The effervescent Harold Arlen-E.Y. Harburg songs, lavish settings (every one—outdoor and indoor—on studio sound stages), fantastic make-up and costumes that did not smother the actors' own physical characteristics (as had those in the failed, all-star *Alice in Wonderland*), ingenious special effects—all remain high-watermark triumphs.

And the story, with its cozy, old-fashioned proverbs framed in timeless flights of fancy. . . .

The Wizard of Oz opens as Dorothy Gale tries to convince her guardians, Auntie Em and Uncle Henry (Clara Blandick and Charley Grapewin), that vinegary, influential Elvira Gulch (Miss Hamilton) plans to do something terrible to Dorothy's small terrier, Toto, for chasing her cat. But farm chores have first call on the attention of the elderly couple. Hunk (Bolger), a hired man, can only counsel Dorothy, prophetically, to use her brains; another hand, Hickory (Haley), preoccupied with "tinkering," is no help either. Third farm worker Zeke (Lahr) advises the distraught girl to have courage as he feeds the pigs ("Get in there before I make a dime bank outta ya!"). When she topples off the fence into the pig sty with a shriek, Zeke almost faints from fright.

"Find a place where you won't get in trouble," admonishes her harried aunt, cueing Dorothy's "Over the Rainbow" plaint. She meanders from bale of hay to old wheel to discarded buggy, hugging Toto as she vocalizes her yearning to be "someplace where there isn't any trouble"—"Somewhere over the rainbow, bluebirds fly/Birds fly over the rainbow, why then, oh why, can't I?" Songbirds trill as sunbeams pierce clouds "where troubles melt like lemon drops/Away above the chimney tops" in this simply staged-and-performed historic interlude.

The hatchet-faced Miss Gulch is then shown riding her bicycle pell-mell toward the farm. "I'm all but lame for the bite on my leg," she complains to Dorothy's aunt and uncle, presenting a sheriff's order to take Toto. "You wicked old witch!" blurts the youngster as her pup is stuffed into Miss Gulch's basket. As they drive off, Toto slips out and runs back to Dorothy. She decides to run away, too.

With Toto in tow, she trudges down a lonely dirt road until she encounters Professor Marvel (Morgan), a bogus but kindly clairvoyant roasting wieners while his wagon rests in a ravine. After several guesses, he miraculously divines that she is running away; sneaking a look at a photo in her basket, he further reports the vision of a

060-183

careworn farm woman crying, then putting a
hand to her heart. Worried, Dorothy says
she'd better get home. A storm looms.

A long shot discloses a devastating twister;
closer, chickens and farm hands scurrying for
cover as Auntie Em repeatedly shouts
"Dorothy!" After they have taken refuge in
the cyclone cellar, Dorothy returns. The storm
grows worse—when she opens the front door,
it blows away. In her bedroom, the window
flies off and strikes her on the head, knocking
her unconscious on the bed. The farm house

18

whirls into the sky, and Dorothy, now looking
out the large window, sees a chicken coop float
by, as well as an old lady knitting (Dorothy
waves timorously), a cow, two men rowing a
boat and, finally, Miss Gulch, pedaling her
bike through the air but suddenly trans-
formed into the whooping Witch on a broomstick. When the furiously twisting house finally lands, Dorothy is uninjured. Stillness
prevails. When she opens the door, the movie
is in breath-catching Technicolor and she is in
Munchkinland, a tranquil but topsy-turvy

marzipan world of oversize flowers and tiny thatched huts.

"We must be over the rainbow!" she marvels, clutching Toto.

In a minute a rainbow-hued bubble wafts toward Dorothy, growing bigger and bigger until Glinda (Billie Burke), the lavishly-gowned, titian-tressed Good Witch of the North, glides out. (Glinda is the only major character in Dorothy's fantasy who does not have a prototype back in Kansas.) She points out that Dorothy's house has fallen on the

Wicked Witch of the East (whose feet can be seen sticking out from beneath the dwelling), freeing the Munchkins from her power, and she carols her part in the multi-layered piece, "Munchkinland" ("Come Out, Come Out, Wherever You Are")—dubbed by one Lorraine Bridges, whose Burke-like tremolo here is one of Hollywood's most remarkable, undetectable and little-known examples of "ghost" singing. Gradually, the giggling little people called Munchkins (and that was how the film billed them—most were midgets)

creep forth, their dignitaries proclaiming Dorothy a heroine. As she rides in a carriage around the square, they proclaim: "Ding-Dong! The Witch is Dead!" All the Munchkins are aroused (some from nests, where they sleep in large egg shells!) for a musical celebration in Dorothy's honor. The entertainment features their toylike army in dress parade, along with more personal welcomes from three tiny-voiced, toe-dancing female sprites in pink representing the Lullabye League and another trio of tap-

dancing little toughs from the Lollipop Guild.

The festivities end when, from a burst of red smoke, the Wicked Witch of the West materializes, green-complected and shrouded in black, enraged over her sister's death and the transferal of the late Witch's enchanted ruby slippers to Dorothy's feet.

"I'll get you, my pretty—and your little dog, too! Ah-hah-hah-hah-hah-hah!" she cackles blood-curdlingly, departing in another flaming explosion.

With a witch pursuing her, Dorothy thinks

she had better go back to Kansas—but how? Glinda tells her that only the all-powerful Wizard of Oz can help, and that she will have to go to the Emerald City to see him. "Follow the Yellow Brick Road," instructs Glinda, the Munchkins raising their voices to chorus that caution. Glinda disappears in her globular vehicle, leaving Dorothy to observe, "My, people come and go so quickly around here!"

The Munchkins and Dorothy sing "We're Off to See the Wizard" as Dorothy skips along the Yellow Brick Road which quickly leads to a fork. Nearby, in a field of shiny green cornstalks, a Scarecrow speaks to give her directions. She helps him off his pole and, unsure on his feet, he falls, scattering a little of his straw stuffing. "Oops," he laughs, "there goes some of me again." His head an old sack, he laments that he is too dumb even to scare crows, singing and loose-limbedly jigging "If I Only Had a Brain," until he loses more straw and finally his balance. "Why, if our scarecrows back in Kansas could do *that* our crows would be scared to pieces," comforts

The Witch tosses a ball of fire at the straw man.

Dorothy. He elects to go with her to see the Wizard of Oz in the hope of getting a brain. The odd couple marches down the Yellow Brick Road, the straw man still so wobbly-legged that Dorothy has to keep pulling him up from the rear.

In a fecund orchard, they try to take apples from trees that, under the Wicked Witch's sorcery, suddenly take on human character-istics and turn hostile. Dorothy and the Scare-crow outsmart them by taunting the trees into throwing their fruit at them.

The silver-faced Tin Woodman, rusted im-mobile on the roadside in his raffishly cocked funnel cap, is next on their itinerary. A year before, he explains after they have oiled him back into action, he had been chopping a tree when it rained. He hasn't been able to move since. He, too, has a problem: banging a hollow tin chest, he sighs, "The tinsmith forgot to give me a heart." After clanking through "If I Only Had a Heart," the Tin Woodman makes it three for the Yellow Brick Road. Just then, the Witch shows up on his cabin roof, threatening to make a beehive out of him and to stuff a mattress with the Scarecrow. As a parting gesture, she tosses a ball of fire that singes the straw man. This makes them more determined than ever to see the Wizard of Oz.

"It's funny," muses Dorothy. "I feel as if I'd known you all the time."

In a "dark, creepy" forest, the Cowardly Lion makes his belated entrance, bounding into their path with a roar that sounds suspiciously like Bert Lahr's trademark "Gnong-gnong," followed by a conclusive "Put 'em up, put 'em *uuuuup*!" (His costume: a baggy Doctor Denton-type lion suit with a tail that seems to have a life of its own, plus a slightly matted mane from which peeks two shell-like ears.) The three travelers cower while the Cowardly Lion continues his bluff with a "ruff," taunting the tin man with "How long can you stay fresh in that can?" But when he takes off after Toto, Dorothy slaps his face, and he begins to sob. As he dabs at his tear-filled eyes with the tip of his tail

("Is my nose bleedin'?"), she perceives, "Why you're nothing but a great big coward." Whereupon the Lion performs, "If I Only Had the Nerve" ("I'm afraid there's no denyin'/I'm just a dandy-lion"). Dorothy explains their mission, urging him to join them to seek courage. The Lion accedes, and they all break into "We're Off to See the Wizard."

Just as they behold the gleaming Art Deco Emerald City in the distance, the Wicked Witch puts them to sleep in a rolling poppy field. A superimposed Glinda counteracts with a light snow that wakens the sojourners. As they scamper for the city, the group known as the Rhythmettes chirps the piece known as "Optimistic Voices" ("You're-out-of-the-woods, you're-out-of-the-dark," etc.) on the sound track.

The Emerald City gateman (Frank Morgan again—this time with a large, neatly curled mustache) tells them "no one has ever seen the great Oz"; but when Dorothy displays her magic ruby slippers, he capitulates. ("That's a horse of a different color!") They enter to a rousing march, "Gates of Emerald City," and a Cockney-sounding coachman (another Morgan incarnation) drives them through the city pulled by a white horse that turns purple, red and yellow as everyone belts out "The Merry Old Land of Oz." After a freshening-up at the local Elizabeth Arden's (Dorothy and the Lion get permanents, the Scarecrow new straw, the Tin Woodman a buffing), the Witch reappears to sky-write via broom, "SURRENDER DOROTHY."

"Who's *h-h-her*?" wails the Cowardly Lion, a red bow now pertly atop his quivering head.

Rushing to the Wizard's palace, they are stopped by the guard (Morgan again, now behind a bushy, drooping mustache) whom they soon win over. As they await word from within, the Cowardly Lion delivers the film's cleverest, funniest number, "If I Were King of the Forest" ("Not queen, not duke, not prince"). His three subjects wrap the strutting beast in a royal-looking rug and crown him with a jagged, broken flower pot as he sings, "Each rabbit would show respect to me/Each chipmunk genuflect to me," going on to ask (and answer) the musical question, "What makes the Hottentot so hot? . . . *Courage!*"

The Wizard agrees to an audience. They march down a long green corridor ("Tell me when it's over," Lahr wails, covering his eyes) to witness the Wizard's enlarged-cerebrum head (a well-disguised Morgan), sans body, appearing from roaring flames over an altar. He thunders that he would grant all their requests, but first they have to bring him the broomstick of the Witch of the West.

The next scene takes place in the Haunted Forest of eerie bird cries and gnarled trees with gargoyle faces; one sign reads "I'd Turn Back If I Were You." The intrepid quartet, stalking the wild Witch with giant wrench, net, and spray gun of Witch Remover are suddenly beseiged by her horde of ugly Winged Monkeys who carry off Dorothy and Toto to the "Witch's Castle—1 Mile." Toto escapes, however, as Dorothy cries "I'm frightened!" by the Witch's large crystal ball—horrifiedly viewing therein her anguished Auntie Em abruptly change into the screeching Witch. Toto leads the Scarecrow, the Tin Woodman and the Cowardly Lion to the castle, up mountains which they scale by clinging to the Lion's tail ("I hope my strength holds out," grunts the animal). In purloined guard uniforms (with the Lion's tail protruding), they force their way past the Witch's Cossack-like, enslaved, green-skinned sentinels who chant the dirgelike "March of the Winkies." Guiding Dorothy out of the castle, they are confronted by the Witch whom Dorothy accidentally dissolves when she throws a pail of water on her.

"I'm melting! I'm melting!" the Witch screams, her cries trailing off as she slowly disappears into the floor, leaving only a pile of vaporous clothes.

"You liquidated her, eh?" comments the Wizard when they bring him the broom. Unexpectedly, Toto pulls away the curtain around a small booth to expose a very mortal man furiously working controls. The Wizard (in reality, now seen to be a white-maned Morgan with built-up apple cheeks) is a fraud. Talking and acting fast, he bestows upon the Scarecrow a diploma, certifying a brain; the Cowardly Lion, a medal for bravery ("Shucks, folks, I'm speechless"); and the Tin Woodman, a testimonial-clock shaped like a red heart. "Remember, my sentimental friend," says the Wizard, "you will be judged not by how much you love, but by how much you *are* loved." He goes on to divulge that he was a balloonist from a Kansas fair who had been blown to Oz, where he was acclaimed the Wizard.

"Times being what they were, I accepted the job," he shrugs.

The Wizard still has his balloon and promises to take Dorothy back to Kansas. The Emerald City's square is crowded with people ready to wave them off, but Dorothy, chasing Toto at the last minute, misses the ascension; the Wizard has to fly away without her. Although her three dear friends beg her to stay, Dorothy, homesick, still wants to go. Glinda then bubbles by again, informing Dorothy that she has had the power to return to Kansas all along. Now that she realizes everything she could ever want is right in her own backyard, her charmed ruby slippers will carry her back. Dorothy bids tearful goodbyes to the Cowardly Lion, the Tin Woodman (who remarks, "Now I know I have a heart, because it's breaking") and to the Scarecrow, whispering, "I think I'll miss you most of all." She taps her heels together three times. In her Kansas bedroom and a Sepia world that would never look quite the same again, she revives, a compress on her forehead—the Miss Gulch-Toto crisis of the first reel unresolved, however. (Sticklers, think back.) The three familiar hired hands, her aunt and uncle and even Professor Marvel, passing by the window, are gathered around her as she expounds excitedly on the wonders of the Land of Oz.

But, at last: "Oh, Auntie Em, there's *no* place like home!"

The film fades out on Dorothy's/Judy's radiant face.

The Wizard of Oz made its players immortal. Judy, of course, inevitably—all eager raw talent. Ray Bolger, his nimble, lean body and cheerful, open, bumpkin manner superbly meeting the challenges of a unique comic dancing role (which should have allowed more of his latter specialty). Jack Haley, the hapless minstrel, touching as well as droll in probably the least showy of the main parts. Margaret Hamilton, up from battle-ax bits as the matchlessly evil personification of every child's nightmares. Billie Burke, certainly the Hollywood Actress Most Transportable by Bubble, mature but aglitter as the Good Witch—if not exactly fairy princess-like, every inch fairy queen mother-like. And Frank Morgan, winningly adept in his myriad of roles—the mannered, windy sputterings effected in some other pictures kept in check by, perhaps, the director.

Best of all: beady-eyed, bewhiskered Bert Lahr in the only film role that adequately utilized his great burlesque/vaudeville/Broadway-trained comic genius. He used every trick and "schtick" he had learned over the years, and much of his dialogue was so deeply in the Lahr vein of humor that he *had* to have interpolated it himself.

"Unusual weather we're having lately, ain't it?" quipped an unmistakably Lahr Lion, waking during the poppy field snow flurry.

There was pathos and warmth and no little courage in his hirsute buffoon, making Dorothy's partiality to the Scarecrow a bit startling, even briefly unsympathetic. (Although, this late confession of hers did at

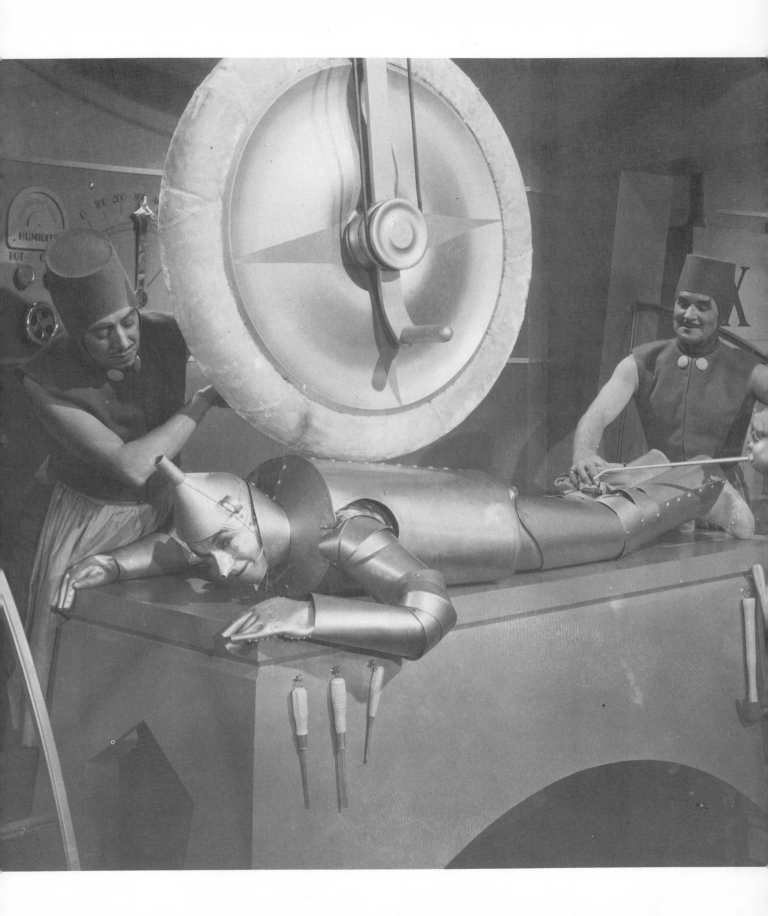

least seem proof that the Cowardly Lion's theft of the film was unintended by anyone save Lahr.) His highpoint, "If I Were King of the Forest," a brilliant parody of the hallowed baritone solo, was also the brightest, rightest number in a score that eschewed the then-usual stop-plot song injections in favor of tunes that advanced the story. In short, a classic melding of clown and character.

The fable is generally hailed first for its spectacle and vision, but it is a very funny, uncondescending picture, too. Almost all the principal characters had senses of humor. Dorothy sweetly delivered lines that in

Dorothy is about to leave for Kansas with the Wizard . . .

But the balloon ascends without Dorothy . . .

. . . leaving Dorothy in Oz
with her friends (temporarily).

"Oh, Auntie Em, there's *no* place like home!"

Glinda and Dorothy

"Unusual weather we're having lately, ain't it?"

calloused hands might have been effective wisecracks, yet she still got chuckles with them. Even the Good Witch, after one of the Wicked Witch's fiery exits, could quail, "What a smell of sulphur!" One-liners were present, much thanks, undoubtedly, to Lahr whose dialect—often sounding as if his Lion had escaped from the Bronx Zoo—was also employed for yocks.* Puns turned up. There was no heavy sense of coping with a classic, no pretentious effort to be other-worldly esoteric in the levity; the writers—and the improvisors—took a breezily contemporary, slangy, sometimes low-comedy approach that, like the other miracles of the production, has not dated—maybe even has gained in nostaligic charm with the years. Only the wheeze uttered after the Winged Monkeys had scattered the Scarecrow's stuffing strains allegiance: "That's you all over!"

The belief that there is no place like home has since come under some fire in certain quarters. Nearly everyone agrees, however, that there is no other film like *The Wizard of Oz*.

*In another time, another medium, Lahr sued a TV cartoon series that was using a voice similar to his for its lion character, and restrained them from doing so.

Low comedy in Oz. The Lion invites everyone to "put 'em up, put 'em up!"

The Wicked Witch and one of her Winged Monkeys

The Book 2

The 1939 motion picture of *The Wizard of Oz* inventively distilled the essence of L. Frank Baum's still beguiling, copiously fanciful 1900 book, but there were many differences between the two.

No suggestion is made in the book of Dorothy's trip over the rainbow being a dream, and the Wicked Witch of the West is a lesser, more stationary character with one eye. In only a few paragraphs, the original work dispatches an equally barren Kansas, where, as one *Wizard of Oz* movie-viewer was especially surprised to read, there reside no counterparts (the farm hands, etc.) to Dorothy's wonderland friends and foes. The Oz lives of the Scarecrow, the Tin Woodman and the Cowardly Lion before Dorothy appears are explored in much greater detail by Baum; furthermore, he creates the questing threesome with healthy deposits of brains, heart and courage, obviously needing no Wizard to augment already formidable attributes. Their adventures, too, are more plentiful and bizarre than those in the movie, and frequently extremely violent. They encounter vicious wolves, crows, bees, likewise the weird Kalidahs (part-bear, part-tiger) and Hammer-Heads (armless beings whose flat domes could be lethal weapons), the author evidencing a strange affinity for decapitations—in a children's book, yet. The Wizard has no set image as he did in the film, but manifests himself to the four wayfarers as, in turn, a great Head, a lovely Lady, a terrible Beast, a Ball of Fire, a solemn Voice and, finally, the old Humbug—perhaps providing the idea that evolved into Hollywood's Frank Morgan playing six disparate characters.

In one oddly untidy bit of business, the book's Dorothy, while anxious to return to Kansas, seems forever taking time out to curl up and sleep on her Yellow Brick Road travels. This might be construed as writer Baum's subtle way of suggesting to tender-aged readers that it was time to close the book for that evening.

Born in Chittenango, New York, on May 15, 1856, the young Lyman Frank Baum was a prolific writer and newspaper-magazine editor who also had tried his hand at acting. Hoping to create a uniquely American fairy tale, one with as little obeisance as possible to the traditional European stories, he set *The Wonderful Wizard of Oz* (his most renowned work's original title, and a phrase from the movie's song "We're Off to See the Wizard") in the heart of the American prairie. The book, which came close to being called *The Emerald City* and for a while before publica-

A scene from the 1925 silent version of
THE WIZARD OF OZ. With Oliver Hardy,
Dorothy Dwan, and Larry Semon

tion was *From Kansas to Fairyland*, caught on immediately. By the time the 1939 film version was underway, it had been read by an estimated 80,000,000 people. Interestingly, the illustrator, W.W. Denslow, earned more kudos from the critics of the day than author Baum.

The book was followed three years later, in 1903, by a Broadway stage version with libretto and lyrics by Baum, music by Paul Tietjens and A. Baldwin Sloane. *The Wizard of Oz* was the debut production for New York's Majestic Theatre, and an auspicious one: widely praised and imitated, it ran for 293 performances, elevating two vaudeville veterans named Fred Stone and Dave Montgomery to stardom as the Scarecrow and the Tin Woodman. Anna Laughlin was Dorothy—carried to Oz by the cyclone with her pet cow! The show eventually toured almost a thousand American cities. Baum, who had never meant his Oz characters to monopolize his career as they did, wrote thirteen more Oz stories literally by public demand, beginning with *The Marvelous Land of Oz*. There were also non-Oz nursery rhymes featuring a character named Father Goose, as well as many other juvenile-oriented books, plus some adult-aimed novels. Eight of Baum's Oz yarns were staged during his lifetime.

Late in this century's first decade, he trouped with one of the earliest examples of mixed-media performances, which he called "radio plays" (named before that aural device was so designated). Baum related his Oz tales on stage while silent picturizations shot by the Selig Company, a moving picture pioneer, were shown on the large screen alongside him. The first film of *The Wizard of Oz*, a Selig one-reeler in 1910, occasioned no stir.

Baum and his wife, hoping by 1911 to live the quiet life, came upon a sleepy California town where they built a grey frame house called Ozcot. The town was a pre-movie boom Hollywood.

In 1913 Baum formed the Oz Film Company* in Los Angeles. During its two years' existence, the studio made—besides various other features and short subjects—three five-reel, silent Land-of-Oz photoplays. The first was *The Patchwork Girl of Oz*; its resounding thud caused distributors to insist that the second, *The Magic Cloak of Oz*, be cut to two reels for theater "filler" and that the third, *His Majesty, The Scarecrow of Oz*, be re-titled the more commercial-sounding *The New Wizard of Oz*. All failed anyway, although today editor Kathleen Karr in *The American Film Heritage* book has called them "charming . . . primitive, but much more satisfying than the Selig Oz pictures or Larry Semon's 1925 rendition of *The Wizard of Oz*."**

Baum longed for a daughter, whom he would have named Dorothy, but had four sons. He died at his Hollywood, California, home on May 6, 1919. As it might have been Dorothy Gale's, his favorite work nook had been the garden, where he nurtured prize-winning dahlias and (in an aviary) scores of pet songbirds.

---

*Comedian Harold Lloyd and producer-director Hal Roach worked as extras there.

**Released by Chadwick Pictures, funnyman Larry Semon's silent production was co-scripted by the star (who also directed) and L. Frank Baum, Jr. It deviated considerably from Baum, Sr.'s model, with a quite mature Dorothy (Dorothy Dwan) hurled to Oz with three farm hands (Semon, G. Howe Black and a pre-Stan Laurel Oliver Hardy) who were turned into the Scarecrow, the Lion, and the Tin Woodman, respectively, by the Wizard (Charlie Murray). While a Count was the head villain, Semon's re-writing to showcase his own brand of clowning brought a strained effect. This *Wizard* fizzled.

The Casting

Although *The Wizard of Oz* has been called one of the most perfectly cast films ever made, almost all of its principal players were second- and even third-choices. A Good Witch of the West *Coast* seemed to be watching over things.

Judy Garland, inconceivable as it may sound to some, was more or less an afterthought for the role of Dorothy. MGM began to consider the Baum story as a viable film project in 1937, the plan being to borrow top box-office star Shirley Temple from 20th Century-Fox to play the moppet heroine, in turn loaning Metro superstars Clark Gable and Jean Harlow to Fox for studio boss Darryl Zanuck's Chicago fire extravaganza, *In Old Chicago*. Mid-year, however, Harlow died suddenly of uremic poisoning at age twenty-six, and the MGM-Fox trade was off. *In Old Chicago* was made with the Fox lot's own Tyrone Power and Alice Faye.

(20th Century-Fox was never really too keen about loaning its biggest star to another studio, anyway. Instead, in 1940 Zanuck and Fox produced their own expensive *Wizard of Oz*-type fairy tale with Shirley Temple, Maurice Maeterlinck's *The Blue Bird*. It failed, certifying the maturing Shirley's fall from favor at the studio.)

Universal's teen-aged prima donna, Deanna Durbin, was also considered in producer Mervyn LeRoy's studio-pressured quest for a "name," but she was even more nubile-looking than Judy.

Surely a press agent planted Bonita Granville's name in one column as a possibility for Dorothy. The malevolent brat in *These Three* (1936), Bonita, although a year younger than Judy, would have been more believable as the Witch.

Born in 1922 and a mother-dominated trouper since the age of two-and-a-half, Judy Garland had been steadily climbing at Metro since signing there late in 1935. She had done the Broadway Melody-Andy Hardy gambit, impressing everyone with her vibrant personality and incredibly emotional, mature singing voice on numbers like "(Dear Mr. Gable) You Made Me Love You," the standard song revised for her by arranger-vocal coach-composer Roger Edens. Arthur Freed, the ambitious song lyricist (sometimes for Judy) who had induced his friend-employer Louis B. Mayer to buy *The Wizard of Oz* and who assisted Mervyn LeRoy—newly arrived from Warner Brothers—in its making, wanted Judy in the first place, but was told by studio brass that she was not a big enough name. With Temple and Durbin out, Freed, who eventually would produce most of Judy's

55

Judy Garland in her blonde wig during the discarded first two weeks of filming. Also shown: Margaret Hamilton

biggest hits, again pitched for Garland. Backed by Edens and, finally, LeRoy, he got her.

"I reasoned, successfully, that she could sing the part as Shirley never could," Freed said later.

The picture got off to an aborted start, though, during which brief period Judy's Dorothy underwent a felicitous physical metamorphosis. As she herself described it: "They tried to convert me into another person. They put a long blonde wig on me and tried to change my nose, because it dipped in too much, by reinforcing it with putty, and

they put caps all over my teeth. I looked like a male Mary Pickford by the time they got through!"*

Only the caps were retained when shooting resumed.

*Coincidentally (perhaps), virtually the same situation occurred on screen in Judy's 1954 vehicle, A Star is Born, scripted by Moss Hart. About to be screen-tested, band singer Judy is given the once-over by the studio make-up department. "The nose is the problem!," winces one make-up man. To draw attention away from this imperfection, they gussy her up in a blonde wig, layers of make-up, and a putty nose. James Mason, cast as her actor-mentor, laughs incredulously when he sees what has been done to her — then orders it undone.

Judy Garland in a test wig she never wore
in the released version of the film.

Jack Haley as the Tin Woodman

But there were still problems. At sixteen, Judy was filling out fast. Her childish garb had to be designed to conceal this fact by Adrian, who also fashioned a special *haute* corset to bind her breasts. (Adrian would receive more renown for his Joan Crawford shoulder pads than for his Judy Garland corset.) Pigtails were ordered.

Judy, adored by critics and public alike as Dorothy, and honored by the Motion Picture Academy of Arts and Sciences with a miniature Oscar as 1939's outstanding juvenile,* stood almost alone in her dissatisfaction with the results. At least, so the disturbed, then not-always-consistent star expressed herself a few years before her death in 1969. "It's odd but when I see those old pictures I can't quite connect myself with them. I've seen *The Wizard of Oz* a couple of times recently on TV. I think it was a very good picture, but I don't think I was good. I think I was boring. I played that part so many times—acting so darn happy!"

Judy, who developed a sophisticated sense of humor, often referred to her early roles as her "Dorothy Adorable" parts.

The actor initially hired for the Tin Woodman was not Jack Haley but Buddy Ebsen, who, with his sister Vilma, was a popular stage-and-screen dance act. (Starring roles on television's *The Beverly Hillbillies* and *Barnaby Jones* were still years in his future.) He had danced with Judy in her second full-length film, MGM's *Broadway Melody of 1938* (1937). On *Wizard of Oz*, he rehearsed for twelve weeks and pre-recorded all the songs but filmed for only two weeks.

The primary element of Ebsen's make-up was an aluminum facial dust spray (over a clown-white base) which, after he'd inhaled it

*Mickey Rooney, about two years older than Judy, had been nominated that year in the adult Best Actor category for their co-starring vehicle, *Babes in Arms.* Many felt Judy should have been nominated as Best Actress for *The Wizard of Oz.*

Frank Morgan as the Wizard

The Wizard of OZ

by L. Frank Baum

Wallace Beery,
who tested for the role of the Wizard,
shows daughter Carol Ann
some of the publicity art for the film.

1060X

for a while, caused a breathing impairment first thought to be aluminum poisoning in the lungs; he was rushed to the hospital and put in an iron lung. The company (re-grouping, anyway) was forced to replace him. The jaunty Haley, who had worked with Shirley Temple in a couple of Fox films and, earlier, with Judy in her first feature, Fox's *Pigskin Parade* (1936), stepped into Ebsen's part. Make-up chief Jack Dawn this time devised not a spray but a paste of the aluminum dust (tinted with household bluing, the better to get the desired silvery effect) that spread on Haley's face and created no serious difficulties.

Ebsen's bucolic style of performing might have been a little too similar to co-player Ray (Scarecrow) Bolger's, so everything was probably for the best after all.

Both W. C. Fields and Ed Wynn were early choices for the multi-faceted Wizard role(s). Fields reputedly turned it down because the pay was insufficient, Wynn because the part wasn't large enough.

Actually, Fields thought the money very good ($5,000 a day, if one believes a Fields letter recently unearthed by the iconoclastic comedian's grandson; $150,000 in toto, according to other, more realistic sources), but he was too involved in writing his own starring vehicle at Universal, *You Can't Cheat an Honest Man* (1939), to take a supporting assignment even at plush MGM. Later, Fields, with an understandable yelp of "Godfrey Daniels!," must have bee-lined for a libation after going to see the classic he'd passed on—at a time when his career could have used a boost.

Wynn's purported refusal now seems, for whatever reason, apocryphal. True, he had just played the lead—a naive farmer-inventor—in the Arlen-Harburg Broadway musical *Hooray for What?* But since he was known then mainly as the lisping "Perfect Fool" of stage and radio, and since the *Wizard of Oz* engagement would have permitted him

to play the equivalent of six different roles as well as to get an elusive foothold in films, the chance is remote that Wynn would veto the job because it was too small. Beloved, befuddled MGM contract actor Frank Morgan, the *rara avis* who had stolen scenes from Shirley Temple,* was, of course, the lucky third and final choice; he imparted a gentle warmth and a skill to his hectic chores that the previous two contenders could have been expected to miss.

Interestingly, Wallace Beery, then a bigger movie attraction than Fields, Wynn *or* Morgan and signed with MGM, had tested for the Wizard, an assignment he wanted very much. (He had introduced the young Judy Garland on radio when she first signed with Metro.) The powers-that-were decided that "Barnacle Bill's" extravagant personality might overwhelm their blithe fairy tale.

Edna May Oliver was one of the first actresses thought of for the Wicked Witch of the West; but since every moviegoer knew that her imperiously gruff, horse-faced exterior concealed a heart of mush, she was ruled out.

Sleek and slithery movie villainess Gale Sondergaard—winner of the first Supporting Actress Oscar in 1936 for Warner Brothers' *Anthony Adverse* (directed by Mervyn LeRoy) but subsequently blacklisted for years following a witch-hunt of a different nature (McCarthy era investigations)—came *that* close to delineating a very unique Wicked Witch.

Miss Sondergaard, under contract to Metro as *Wizard of Oz* preparations began, recounted her experience to Leonard Maltin in *Film Fan Monthly*: "We actually did the costumes—a high, pointed hat, but of sequins, and a very glamorous sequined gown. She was to be the most glamorous, but wicked sort of Witch. We got into testing for it, and it was absolutely gorgeous. Then, I suppose,

*In *Dimples* (1936).

Margaret Hamilton as
the Wicked Witch of the West

Mervyn got to remembering that this was a classic by now, and the children who read it, and the grown-ups, too, were going to say, 'That isn't the way it was written!' Everybody agreed that you could not do that to *The Wizard of Oz*. And Mervyn said to me, 'I don't want you to be an ugly Witch.' So we dropped the whole thing.''

Margaret Hamilton, a parrot-profiled ex-schoolteacher "character woman," picked up the ball.

It was a familiar one. Once upon a time she'd read the Oz stories to her kindergarten pupils, and she had acted the Witch twice before on the stage. When MGM asked her to test for the role, telling her to use her own conception of the character, she requisitioned some "old rags," a broomstick, and a pointed, sequinless hat from the wardrobe department. Employing her own evil cackle, she made a very unglamorous—but ideal—Witch. Then Gale Sondergaard seemed to have the role, and Miss Hamilton says she resigned herself, as most actresses sooner or later must, to losing a coveted part. She relates that one Saturday afternoon, while attending a football game in Los Angeles with her husband, she ran into producer LeRoy who asked her—"just like that"—if she'd like to be the Witch. Through her agent she requested a guarantee of at least three weeks' work, got a six-week promise, and wound up working for twenty-three weeks on the movie—from fall, 1938, until spring, 1939.

Judy Garland once said that her domineering "stage mother," Mrs. Ethel Gumm, a frustrated ex-performer alleged to have put her talented, infant daughter Frances (much later re-named Judy) to work, would have made the best Wicked Witch of the West of all!

Billie Burke won her favorite movie role by default. Young MGM starlet Helen Gilbert was set for the Good Witch of the North but disappeared on a spree with Howard Hughes,

it was rumored, and was suspended by the studio. Miss Burke, widow of girl-glorifying impresario Florenz Ziegfeld and for generations a celebrated, if flighty-acting, beauty herself, was also on Metro's roster and had no qualms about replacing Miss Gilbert.

At one point it was leaked that May Robson, the lovably cranky, Academy Award-nominated Best Actress of *Lady for a Day* (1933) fame, would play work-weary Auntie Em. Then Miss Robson backed out because she thought the role "lacked meat." Next, it looked like the veteran Janet Beecher was set. When it was weighed that her patrician presence would seem incongruous on a Kansas farm, Clara Blandick, an old-fashioned schoolteacher-type actress with a frozen scowl, was handed her most famous job.

Others prominent in *The Wizard of Oz* were uncontested choices. Ray Bolger, already working at MGM and a comedic hoofer who had been called a combination of Leon (Rubber Legs) Errol and Fred Astaire, was certainly the perfect shimmy-shanked straw man. And grizzled old Charley Grapewin (soon to be the screen's Jeeter Lester in *Tobacco Road* and Inspector Queen in the Ellery Queen series) slipped into the proceedings without incident as the rather shunted aside Uncle Henry. Grapewin had written the book for Arthur Freed's west coast stage musical *Pair o' Fools*.

Early drafts of the *Wizard* script had funny girl/lady Fanny Brice, singers Betty Jayne and Kenny Baker penciled in as a witch, princess and a prince, respectively, characters written out of the final screenplay.

Perhaps significantly, the very first principal to be signed was Bert Lahr, in retrospect lending credence to the lingering impression that a considerable portion of the disarming irreverent picture took cues from his Lion-esque Cowardly Lion. When LeRoy first offered it to Lahr, who LeRoy claimed had never heard of the book, "he thought I was

Ray Bolger as the Scarecrow

Bert Lahr as the Cowardly Lion

crazy," the producer reveals. " 'Me, a *lion?*' he said. . . I knew Bert from our old vaudeville days. Haley and Bolger, too." Then Lahr read the script, which he thought "beautiful." On the set, Frank Morgan, with a wizard's gift of prophecy, told him, "Bert, you're going to be a great hit in this picture. But it's not going to do you a damn bit of good—you're playing an animal." Lahr got the best reviews and succeeding screen roles were indeed dismal.

Wizard of Oz lyricist E. Y. Harburg, who had done a couple of Broadway shows with Lahr, may have been the first person to recognize the extreme compatibility of Lion and Lahr. Pushing for the great stage clown who until then had been only mildly effective in films, he quoted some of the fey beast's dialogue from the script (on which Harburg, uncredited, also helped) to LeRoy and Freed during early conferences, noting its similarity to distinctive Lahr jargon. They agreed that he would be funny, but Harburg knew he would be much more. Today, Harburg says, "A lyricist is lucky to have a Bert Lahr in his lifetime, who incorporates humor and humanity in his performance."

As the Lion himself might remark, "Ain't it de truth, ain't it de *troooooth*!"

The Production 4

*T*he year *The Wizard of Oz* was released, 1939, was also the year of such films as *Gone with the Wind*, *Wuthering Heights*, *Ninotchka*, *Stagecoach*, *Goodbye, Mr. Chips*, *Mr. Smith Goes to Washington*, *The Women*, *Golden Boy*, *Love Affair*, *Of Mice and Men*, *Midnight*, *Destry Rides Again*, *Only Angels Have Wings*, *Gunga Din*, *The Story of Vernon and Irene Castle*, *The Story of Alexander Graham Bell*, *Drums Along the Mohawk*, *Made for Each Other*, *Babes in Arms*, *The Adventures of Huckleberry Finn* and *The Adventures of Sherlock Holmes*.

There were no less than four Bette Davis "suffer" sagas: *The Old Maid* (giving up her child), *The Private Lives of Elizabeth and Essex* (giving up her man), *Juarez* (giving up her sanity), *Dark Victory* (giving up her life). Moviegoers that year probably would not have been surprised to find Bette as Dorothy in *The Wizard of Oz* (giving up her Scarecrow).

Andy Hardy got spring fever, Topper took a trip, Charlie Chan went to Treasure Island, the Cisco Kid returned, Blondie met the boss, Dr. Kildare had a secret, Tarzan found a son, three smart girls grew up, and four daughters became four wives.

The motion picture as an art form—and an industry—was peaking; indeed, many film historians have called 1939 the screen's greatest year. The Depression was ending, talking pictures had had more than a decade to prove they were far from a fad, and the lucrative foreign market was still accessible. World War II budget restrictions and artist-manpower shortages were a couple of years away. The moguls reigned omnipotent. MGM was "the Cadillac of the studios." Nothing, it seemed, was spared to make *The Wizard of Oz* succeed, and nobody considered the expense.

Unless you want to count New York-based Nicholas (Nick) Schenck, president of MGM's parent company Loew's, Inc., and financial ruler of the empire run in Hollywood by the mighty Louis B. Mayer. Half-way through the filming, Schenck complained that producer LeRoy was "ruining the company, spending too much money"—*The Wizard of Oz* would wind up costing the then unprecedented sum of $2,777,000. LeRoy told him, "Mr. Schenck, I wish I had three million, I'd buy it from you. It's going to be worth more than that." Mayer, the great advocate of wholesome motion pictures who, furthermore, had just beguiled LeRoy away from Warner Brothers with an astronomical weekly salary of $6,000, backed up his new producer and shooting continued.

But, as Glinda advised Dorothy when she was in a quandary concerning just where on

73

The costliness of
THE WIZARD OF OZ.
From the "Renovation
Sequence," cut
from the film

Mervyn LeRoy,
Judy Garland,
Victor Fleming,
and the Munchkins

Victor Fleming directs the talking apple trees.

the Yellow Brick Road to begin her mission to the Emerald City, it's always best to begin at the beginning.

In the early thirties, producer Samuel Goldwyn was always seeking vehicles for contract star Eddie Cantor. He asked his new story scout George Oppenheimer to find a property that would lend itself to the Cantor musical comedy approach, and Ozophile writer Oppenheimer suggested the L. Frank

Baum stories. Early in 1934, Goldwyn announced that he had bought most of the Oz stories from Baum's estate and within a few months would start filming *The Wizard of Oz*. When he shortly lost interest in Cantor, he also lost interest in *The Wizard of Oz*.

By 1937, however, the country had grown very fairy-tale conscious in the excitemen created by imminent release of the fir: feature-length cartoon, Walt Disney's *Snot*

Mervyn LeRoy watching the Emerald City arrival scene

The arrival at Emerald City

White and the Seven Dwarfs. People in the motion picture industry already sensed an incipient classic in *Snow White*, and movie fans who hadn't seen it either, but who were snowed by the publicity maelstrom began writing to MGM and other studios pleading with them to produce a similar entertainment. All this coincided with the emergence of Arthur Freed at MGM as a potential producer. He had discussed the matter with Mayer, who consented to allow his songwriting friend—Freed had composed "Singin' in the Rain" with Nacio Herb Brown—to advance himself, *if* the right property came along.

Enter *The Wizard of Oz*. Freed had loved Baum's stories from childhood, felt the original book would make a perfect debut vehicle for his new role as producer and convinced Mayer to buy the rights to the Baum package from Goldwyn for $20,000—one of the best buys since the sale of Manhattan. Naturally, since MGM was not in the animation business, their version would be "a realistic fantasy." The purchase was revealed in February, 1938. Mayer, however, became dubious about launching Freed's new career with a production that even on paper appeared certain to be one of the studio's most expensive.

Enter Mervyn LeRoy. Just lured to MGM from Warner Brothers, where he had directed such prestige successes as *I Am a Fugitive from a Chain Gang* (1932) and *They Won't Forget* (1937), LeRoy was Mayer's choice to produce *Wizard of Oz*. At Metro, LeRoy was producing *Dramatic School* (1938), starring Luise Rainer, which even in the "rushes" (the unprocessed scenes just shot) looked like a dud. Mayer, loath to be proved wrong, thought that the spectacular *Wizard of Oz* would surely bring out the best in LeRoy and justify his faith in his embarrassingly overpaid new employee. But since the film was expected to be one of the toughest assignments

ever handed a producer, Mayer did not want LeRoy to spread himself too thin by directing as well. Freed, promised that it would lead to bigger things, accepted an apprenticeship post of associate producer; but getting (and keeping) a director was to be one of the most critical problems of a picture that was to face unprecedented problems before it was finished.

Norman Taurog, who had a way with children and had just directed the company's *Boys Town* (1938), was the first director considered for *The Wizard of Oz*. When filming began late in September, 1938, however, Richard Thorpe, a journeyman veteran responsible for the thriller *Night Must Fall* (1937), was at the helm, only to be dismissed after about two weeks. LeRoy has said, "Thorpe didn't have the feeling for it. I guess you have to have the heart of a kid to make *The Wizard of Oz*."

Thorpe replies: "I don't believe any of the footage remains made during the few days I was on the picture—Jack Haley replaced Buddy Ebsen as the Tin Woodman at that time, too. It's not the first time a producer has disagreed with a director (especially if the producer is a director), nor will it be the last. I wonder if you know that George Cukor was assigned to the picture a few days before Victor Fleming took it over?"

LeRoy claims that Cukor—the highly sophisticated "woman's director" of, for instance, *The Women* (1939)—"asked out because he didn't understand it."

Cukor says he was never definitely going to direct the picture. He notes that they had been shooting and changes were being made, and that MGM had asked him to make a test of Judy Garland. He immediately disapproved of her make-up. "She looked doll-like, the make-up too heavy—and I think she was wearing a wig. She was, of course, very young at the time. I suggested that they make her look as human and as natural as possible. I

The Witch and her Winged Monkeys

The arrival scene in rehearsal.
Note the studio personnel
through the open door.

The Witch's hour glass explodes before the Winkies.

told Judy that the joke of it was that she was Dorothy from Kansas. She should really look like that and remain that way. Then her meetings with these strange people and her strange adventures would be more telling. The studio did change her make-up, hair, etc., following my ideas. That was my sole connection with it." He remembers Judy as "very intelligent for her age, and very knowledgeable."

84

According to Margaret Hamilton, "It seems to me that Lewis Milestone, who had directed *All Quiet on the Western Front*, was on the film for a while, too. As each director left, we went in for an interview. Each time we thought we'd get the ax, but LeRoy wanted us. Mr. LeRoy had wanted to direct the picture himself, you see, and had very firm ideas about how the thing should be done, and, after all, he *was* the producer."

Ex-cameraman Victor Fleming got the job, keeping *his* favorite cameraman, Harold Rosson. A dashing "man's man" whom Spencer Tracy called "the Clark Gable of the directors," the seasoned Fleming had a reputation for being able to handle technically difficult productions, such as MGM's *Test Pilot* (1938), starring Gable and Tracy, and furthermore had evidenced a sensitive touch with youngsters in that studio's *Captains Courageous* (1937), with Spencer Tracy and little Freddie Bartholomew. He was among the earliest users of the "traveling mike" and "montage" in film. Although Fleming received lone credit as director of *Wizard of Oz*, there was more commotion to come in this crucial area. (The assistant directors were not spared, either: seven came and went.)

The screenplay was one of the first hurdles. Herbert Fields, Herman J. Mankiewicz and

The Witch about to fly off the parapet

Mervyn LeRoy (standing) and Victor Fleming (in hat), with the set designers

Irving Brecher were among the initial writers mentioned; then it was decided that Florence Ryerson and Edgar Allan Woolf should prepare a twelve-page "treatment" of the story. On the strength of their outline, Ryerson and Woolf were hired to do the screenplay, and LeRoy brought in Noel Langley "who has a fey quality—he's written fantasy" to work with them. At one point Freed, like everyone else on the production seemingly obsessed

with obtaining "the right fantasy touch," hired Ogden Nash to embellish things. He wrote a four-page précis that proved non-filmic. Ironically, after the film opened, *New York Times* critic Frank S. Nugent wrote, "The nonsense verses sung by Bert Lahr . . . are worthy of Ogden Nash."

Throughout the shooting, particularly in the early stages when LeRoy was still involved with *Dramatic School*, Freed offered suggestions that more often than not were helpful. He was especially strong in the music and script departments, being a lyricist himself, and devised a few of the plot turns that became part of the movie. He was a good editor, keeping the in-progress scenario from becoming too wordy.

The final writing credit on the film: Screenplay by Noel Langley, Florence Ryerson and Edgar Allan Woolf; Adaptation by Noel Langley.

In 1939, Ryerson and Woolf stated:

No screen writer faces a more difficult task than the translation of a classic from the printed word into celluloid, and when the classic is for children, the difficulty is increased because many generations have read and loved that book.

Of all children's books, *The*

Dorothy and Toto at the fork in the Yellow Brick Road

A closer view of the corn fields.
Dorothy meets the Scarecrow.

Wizard of Oz is most widely read, most dearly loved. Hence, we daily received letters from fans warning us to follow the book and to leave out no characters.

Necessarily, a few things had to be sacrificed by selecting the most important incidents and characters and telescoping or combining others. When we had finished, we were amazed to realize how little had been left out. Only a few grotesque things, which might be amusing to read about, but would not be well to look at, were eliminated.

We included Dorothy, the Wizard, the Scarecrow, the Tin Woodman, the Cowardly Lion, the Wicked Witch, Glinda the Good, the Munchkins, the Winkies, the Winged Monkeys, the trees which could take hold of people and the inhabitants of the Emerald City.

Changes in the story were really minor. For example, in the book when the characters are overcome by poison in the poppy field, the field-mouse queen and all her mice rescue the characters. That, of course, couldn't be done on the screen. Instead, we have Glinda the Good send a snow storm to revive them. We also eliminated the wishing cap and have the characters merely seek the Witch's broomstick.

We changed the scenes in the Witch's castle slightly, making them a little more dramatic. But all the episodes are there, including the melting of the Witch and the final scenes where the Wizard proves a humbug and, then being on the spot, is forced to show the charac-ters they really have the qualities they've been wanting. He is still a balloonist and flies away without Dorothy, and she clicks her heels and goes home.

The only change in the ending is in pointing up Baum's philosophy and having Dorothy repeat the words, "There's no place like home." We also stress the Kansas farm sequences more than in the book, but do so to build character only.

We scenarists did have problems. But they were those that involved satisfying Oz readers. We left in the most memorable incidents, never altered the characters; and we inserted most of the magic. After that, it was the problem of those technical geniuses to figure out how to do those strange things. And they did.

Arnold (Buddy) Gillespie, perhaps the doyen of Hollywood's special effects wizards, was in the vanguard of those "technical geniuses." He and sound department chief Douglas Shearer were rewarded for their *Wizard of Oz* work with a joint Oscar nomination in the Academy's brand-new Special Effects category. (E.H. Hansen and Fred Sersen won for *The Rains Came*.)

One of Gillespie's most ingenious achievements was the cyclone. Stumped for a while, he tried several different ways of photographing the great twister that blew Dorothy to Oz. None worked. Finally, in an inspired bit of resourcefulness, he took a woman's silk stocking, set it up with a fan blowing it and shot it. *Voilà*—Dorothy's awesome cyclone that provided MGM with stock storm footage it used for years, in such films as *Cabin in the Sky* (1943).

Another challenge was the army of Winged Monkeys, which the studio originally wanted

90

A rambunctious apple tree

The Tin Man, the Cowardly Lion, and the Scarecrow, masquerading in Adrian's costumes for the Winkies

to do in cartoon animation. "I was a little against it because I thought you would be able to tell it was animation on the screen," explained Gillespie in *Hollywood Speaks*, by Mike Steen. "After a number of tests and experiments, they gave up the idea of animation, and we did it with miniature monkeys we cast and supported with 2,200 piano wires! The wires supported them on an overhead trolley and moved their wings up and down. It

was an awful job to hide the wires. They had to be painted and lighted properly so that they blended into whatever the background might be."

Then there was "the horse of a different color," which had to change colors several times in a few seconds. Since a single steed would have been impractical, the required number of white horses was obtained and the effects department prepared to paint each one a different color. Whereupon the ASPCA stepped in and forbade them to do so. The solution was found by tinting the horses with various flavors of Jello—which, to everyone's consternation, the animals kept licking off.

The traveling bubble from which Glinda stepped forth took three months to create because double exposure could not be done with color in those early days. Her sphere was manufactured with a ballcock from a common household toilet.

On many occasions, stage illusions were necessary and actual magicians were called in to advise. One of these instances was near-tragic. For the Munchkinland scene in which Margaret Hamilton as the Wicked Witch exited in a flaming gust, the stage had been constructed so that Miss Hamilton would stand on a platform that was to lower her six feet by elevator. Tubes containing smoke and fire en-

The Tin Woodman, in his "shiny metallic costume" that "tended to go toward the blue," begins to rust again.

Dorothy in Munchkinland

Certificate of Death

Victor Fleming, Judy Garland, and the Munchkins

circled the platform, the smoke to be released when she stepped on the platform, the fire after she had been lowered.

But it didn't work out quite that way. As Miss Hamilton went down, her hat and broom caught fire, leaving her in "excruciating pain as doctors labored to remove my make-up," she recalls. "The green paint had copper in it. If they hadn't gotten the paint off, my face would have been a mass of holes." Out of the

picture six weeks because of this mishap, she returned to notify MGM, "No more fire work! Release me if you want to, but *no more fire work*! I let go of the idea that the show must go on."

"When they ask how I flew in the movie," she continues, "I tell them I jumped off a fake parapet and the camera cut to a drawn miniature of me sailing off into the sky. As for how I melted, I went down through the floor on an elevator again, leaving some fizzling dry ice and my floor-length costume.''

The art department, headed by Cedric Gibbons, rose to new heights on *The Wizard of Oz*. In a 1965 study of Gibbons' career in *Films in Review*, George P. Erengis wrote:

> It is only in an out-and-out fantasy film that art directors can let their imaginations soar and Gibbons thoroughly enjoyed working on

The Wizard of Oz. That film begins and ends with Sepia-toned scenes of a Kansas farm, and in between is a Technicolored parade of ageless wonders that has not been equalled since. Oz was made of a land of verdant, bubble-like hills, giant waxy blossoms, garrulous apple trees and shimmering cities of emerald. Fortunately, free-wheeling imagination

Dorothy is proclaimed a heroine by the Munchkins.

The Witch and one of her Winged Monkeys

did not stop with the art directing of Gibbons and William A. Horning, but extended into the make-up work of Jack Dawn, the costuming of Adrian and the special effects of Arnold Gillespie, which, among many other wonders, made the Wizard's monstrous head float on top of multi-colored plumes of smoke. Had *The Wizard of Oz* not been up against the stiff competition of *Gone with the Wind* that

year, it would surely have brought Gibbons his third Oscar.*

*The following films won Academy Awards for Cedric Gibbons and his MGM art department: *The Bridge of San Luis Rey* (1929); *The Merry Widow* (1934), shared with Frederic Hope; *Pride and Prejudice* (1940), with Paul Groesse; *Blossoms in the Dust* (1941), with Urie McCleary; *Gaslight* (1944), with William Ferrari; *The Yearling* (1946), with Paul Groesse; *Little Women* (1949), with Paul Groesse; *An American in Paris* (1951), with Preston Ames; *The Bad and the Beautiful* (1952), with Edward Carfagno; *Julius Caesar* (1953), with Edward Carfagno; *Somebody Up There Likes Me* (1956), with Malcolm Brown.

Bill Horning was the film's associate art director, working, too, with sketch artist Jack Martin Smith and set decorator Edwin B. Willis. Their main job was, of course, the Land of Oz sets, which, when built, would have covered twenty-five acres of Culver City back lot if they had all been up at the same time. All of MGM's twenty-nine sound stages were ultimately used. There were sixty-five different sets in the film, and because of their bizarre nature relatively few of them were recyclable. Among the more recognizable exceptions was the ravine where Frank Morgan's Professor Marvel was encamped: later in 1939, this setting showed up again as part of the road to Tara in *Gone with the Wind*.

The more modest yet nonetheless striking Kansas prairie designs, with their endless lines of marching telephone poles and zig-zagging fences, were inspired by Grant Wood

A Munchkin player collects the day's wardrobe.

paintings and were not a little daring in their faintly unrealistic style. Thirty-five years later, director Martin Scorsese and writer Robert Getchell opened their film *Alice Doesn't Live Here Anymore* with a flashback to a similar arid, stylized farm setting to show their housewife heroine (Ellen Burstyn) when she was a little girl who, like Dorothy, sang and dreamed of going over the rainbow (to fame as a singer); but—a sign of the times—their child spoke in obscenities against a blazing red sunset.

Surprisingly troublesome on *Wizard* was the simple-seeming task of preparing the Yellow Brick Road—that thoroughfare which has since slipped into the language as facilely as the expression "up the creek," becoming, oppositely, synonymous with all peoples' dreams and aspirations. All kinds of exotic paints and dyes and fancy bricks were tried, but none of them photographed the bright, true yellow needed. Then one morning producer LeRoy suggested to Gibbons that he try some regular, cheap yellow fence paint. This done, the Yellow Brick Road was finally ready for traversing. (The primary element in the interior of the Emerald City was green glass; the budget would stretch only so far).

Other unusual art department achievements:

The sleep-inducing poppy field. Covering an acre-and-a-half of sound stage, it contained 40,000 red poppies with two-foot wire stems which twenty men worked a week sticking in the set.

The rambunctious apple trees. They were constructed of rubber, with men working them from inside. An unbilled actor named Abe Dinovitch was the harsh voice of their ringleader.

Adrian designed 4,000 costumes for the more than 1,000 members of the cast, working closely with the art department because many of the materials had to be tested for color.

LeRoy says it was his idea to film the open-ing and closing scenes in Sepia and the Oz trip in Technicolor, confessing that there were times he wished he'd never thought of it: "The make-up had to be different for the black-and-white portions, but that was a relatively minor matter. What caused the biggest difficulty was the actual moment of transition. Each frame of film had to be hand-painted to make the change from black-and-white to color a smooth one."

In those early years for Technicolor, a lot of experimenting went on in *The Wizard of Oz*, much of it in preparation for the colossal *Gone with the Wind*, produced by David O. Selznick—who had bought into the Technicolor Corporation. The arranging of shooting schedules was a hassle because Technicolor cameras were still in limited supply. (Most of the Sepia scenes were shot last.)

Cinematographer Harold Rosson recalls:

Chief problems were in the characters themselves, especially when there were so many of them in one scene. Margaret Hamilton, as the Wicked Witch, wore black, with hands and face a bright green. We usually kept her before a dark grey background and lighted her black costume brilliantly. Jack Haley as the Tin Woodman, in shining metallic costume, had a tendency to go toward the blue, as light reflected from his outfit. We carefully straw-yellow filtered his lighting. Judy Garland's ruby slippers, with their red sequins, tended to give off sparks of reflection, hence we had to avoid any light shining on them from any angle which would project it into the camera. Billie Burke's brilliant headdress as the Good Witch presented a similar problem. And Frank Morgan's accentuated make-up as the Wizard sometimes gave us

At a rehearsal, Judy Garland exchanges Dorothy's ruby red slippers for the more comfortable household variety!

Judy Garland and Ray Bolger, working under 1000-candle lights

shiny cheekbones to battle with. Putting all these characters together involved much time and care in working out our angles.

Probably the most difficult set to photograph was Munchkinland, a two-acre set of tiny villages, with more than a hundred tiny homes for the midgets. It contained dozens of shades of primary colors. We found it best to try no novel colors but to get variety in shades. The huge set used much light, in fact enough to light 550 five-room homes.

Douglas Shearer's sound department achieved some of the weirdest effects of all. When the director and producer wanted bird calls unlike any ever heard before for the Haunted Forest scene, a crew went to the island of Catalina, where there reportedly were 8,000 birds. They made 15,000 feet of sound track with these birds. Back at the studio, they set about combining two and more bird calls into a single sound, while running other bird sounds backward.

"Disney can thank Christ his Seven Dwarfs weren't real!" groaned one member of MGM's publicity department after months of trying to cope with the swarm of midgets who portrayed the Munchkins and sundry diminutives in *The Wizard of Oz*. The little people were probably the production's biggest headache.

Three hundred and fifty midgets were needed for the picture. When casting director Billy Grady reached the famous Leo Singer of Singer's Midgets, he found that Singer (who was normal size) could provide only a hundred and fifty. So a midget monologist named Major Doyle was contacted to make up the difference. Doyle said he could get Grady the entire three hundred and fifty but that he wouldn't give him *one* if he did business with Singer, who not only had refused Doyle work

on numerous occasions but also, Doyle felt, exploited his employees. Grady explained that he had already promised Singer; Doyle was obdurate. So Grady bowed out of his arrangement with a livid Leo Singer,* and when he told Doyle in front of Dinty Moore's Restaurant in New York, the Major did an Irish jig right there on the sidewalk.

Major Doyle gathered his midgets from all over the world. Buses were hired to transport a hundred and seventy of them from New York to California, the remaining number to be picked up en route. The meeting place was a hotel on West Forty-third Street. Before they got to the Holland Tunnel, however, Major Doyle had re-routed three buses to go by Leo Singer's apartment building at Eighty-eighth Street and Central Park West. They stopped, and Doyle sent word upstairs for Singer to look out his fifth floor window. When Singer appeared, he saw three busloads of midgets with their bare behinds sticking out the windows. The incident became known intracompany as "Major Doyle's Revenge."

It was even worse in Hollywood. In his autobiography, *Take One*, Mervyn LeRoy related: "We kept them in a Culver City hotel. I guess it's like any group who go to a convention in a distant city; somehow, their inhibitions are left behind. Or maybe the little people, as they prefer to be called, have little inhibitions to go with their little stature. Whatever the reason, they were wild. Every night there were fights and orgies and all kinds of carryings-on. Almost every night, the Culver City police had to rush over to the hotel to keep them from killing each other."

Judy Garland always said the authorities "had to scoop them up in butterfly nets."

"The polyglot group of little people came

---

*Perhaps in some compensatory arrangement, much of the *Wizard of Oz* publicity referred to the little people as Singer's Midgets, although they were billed on screen as the Munchkins.

Mickey Rooney visits Ray Bolger on the set.

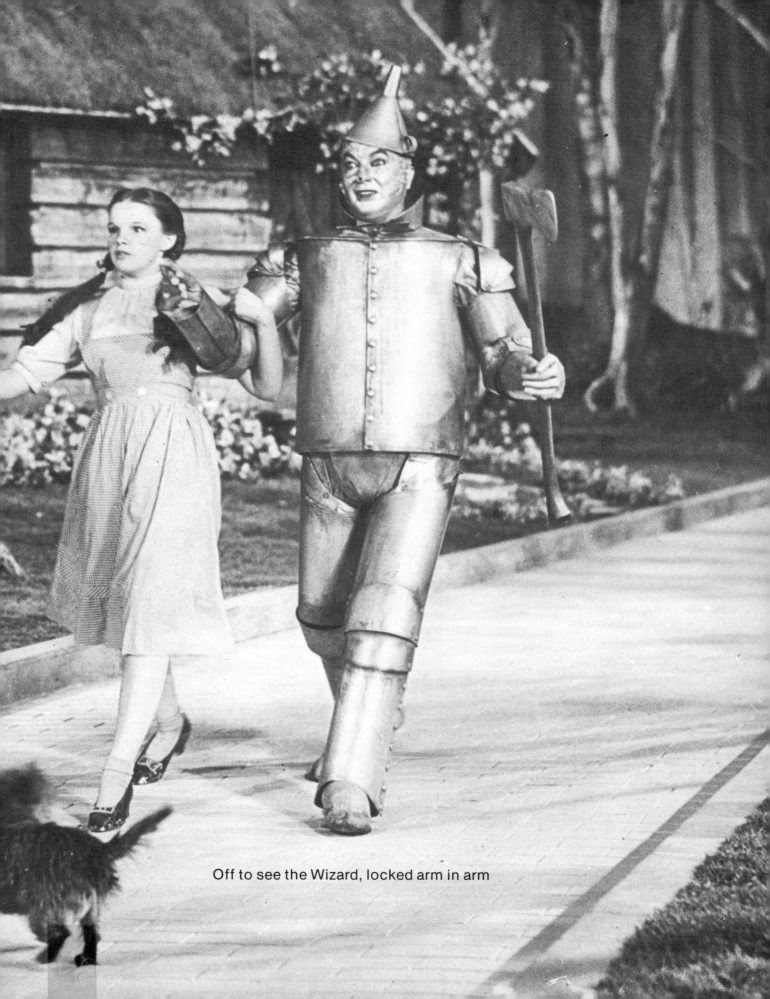

Off to see the Wizard, locked arm in arm

from a wide range of professions," wrote John Lahr in his biography of his father, Bert Lahr, *Notes on a Cowardly Lion*. "Many of the Munchkins were midgets who, in fact, made their living by panhandling, pimping and whoring. Assistants were ordered to watch the crew of midgets, who brandished knives and often conceived passions for other, larger Metro personnel."

The small men pinched Judy's derrière, some even propositioned her. One more prosaic midget asked her for a date. "What could I say?" Judy once shrugged. " 'I don't want to go out with you because you're short?' So I said, 'No, I don't think my mother would let me.' So he said, 'Aw, bring your mom along, too!' "

Full-size men and women, so the story went, had to be stationed in the toilets to lift the tiny people off and on the seats. Bert Lahr told of one day when the men's room attendant took a calamitous long lunch. "We were supposed to shoot a scene with the Witch's Monkeys. The head of the group was a little man called the Count. He was never sober. When the call came, everybody was looking for the Count. We could not start without him. And then, a little ways off stage, we heard what sounded like a whine coming from the men's room. Somebody investigated. They found the Count. He got plastered during lunch, and fell in the latrine and couldn't get himself out."

The Winged Monkeys were to be paid $25 a take every time they swooped down on their wires to attack Dorothy and her friends in the woods. "After the first take," recalls Ray Bolger, "Victor Fleming, the director, yelled, 'Take 'em up again!' That meant $25 more. Then they went up a third time. Another $25. A fourth time. We could hear them saying to each other, 'They'll never pay us all this money. *Never!*' To make sure Metro did fork over the cash, the midgets struck the picture. Stopped it cold for a while."

Musical-numbers director Bobby Connolly, recruited from Broadway's Ziegfeld Follies by way of Warner Brothers and through the years the most neglected of contributors to the film's success, has said, "The toughest job was training a hundred and sixteen midgets to dance. Most of them knew nothing about dancing. We laid out chalk lines on the stage floor to guide them in getting into position for formations. We trained them for days in a lockstep to practice keeping time to music. Then we went into individual steps."

Only a third of the midgets spoke English, and then frequently—as Jack Haley put it—"mit de Cherman agzent"; so well-known "voice animators" like Billy Bletcher and Pinto Colvig were called in to speak (and sing) some of their roles. For the Munchkins, Adrian designed over a hundred individual costumes, each different, each created from a colored sketch. He had to emphasize their smallness. Huge vests and coats and jewelry did it for the men. Each day, twenty of Jack Dawn's make-up men dispatched the Munchkins at the rate of nine an hour. When any of the fringe midgets were "detained" for any reason, adults who simply were a little short for their ages were scrounged to replace them in the scene. Unverified, but not unlikely, are reports that children, too, sometimes acted as ringers here and there.

When cameraman Rosson complained to director Fleming, who seemed to thrive on adversity, that the Munchkins' size and the vivid hues of their costumes were turning them into "a mass of nothing when they all mob together," Fleming came up with the "rubber lens" camera. Fixed on a Chapman boom, or crane, it floated about the action to avoid the running together of colors as well as the better to catch all the players' motions and expressions.

Mervyn LeRoy, known to be kind and tolerant to a fault, admitted recently, "I was very happy when their [the midgets'] part in

A close view of Ray Bolger's Scarecrow make-up

the picture was over."

Although there were warning signs of the personal disequilibrium that would haunt, and finally take, her life (at the age of forty-seven), by most accounts making *The Wizard of Oz* was one of Judy Garland's happier film experiences. She had just received a raise of $150 a week, bringing her salary up to $500 per week.* Dorothy was a coveted role that was almost certain to make her a major star. The extraordinary nature of the story made coming to work a daily adventure, and she seemed to like her colleagues. And they liked her.

Describing the rigors of making this difficult picture to interviewer Jerry Vermilye in *The Movie Buff's Book*, Margaret Hamilton affirmed: "The one who kept us all going was Judy Garland. Her freshness and vitality are things I will never forget. And wonderful Victor Fleming, the director, worked harder than any man I have ever seen to make that film the best of its kind . . . I would imagine that no one in that cast ever worked that hard again. Each day seemed harder than the one before, but we all cared so much about the film that we tried not to let our fatigue show through. The worst for me was the make-up for the Witch. It was deathly hot under the lights, and I couldn't go too long without nearly perspiring it all off." Ray Bolger, Bert Lahr and Jack Haley all had the same kind of problems, she said.

Bolger concurred. "We worked very hard. We had respiratory problems. We used what they call 1,000-candle lights. They don't use them anymore, but they were unbearably hot. If we couldn't have laughed, we would have been tearing each other apart."

During the interminable waits between

*Judy's paycheck was paltry, though, next to her friend and inevitable Metro co-star Mickey Rooney's nearly $5,000 a week. Furthermore, it was shared with her mother, now on MGM's payroll as her coach and manager.

scenes, the Scarecrow, the Tin Woodman and the Cowardly Lion—troupers and cronies from way back—would tease each other to keep their morale up. The somewhat less extraverted Bolger, who tried for a time to keep up with Lahr and Haley by innocently boasting that he had done first whatever they happened to be contemplating, soon took considerable ribbing from the other two. Unlike more serious Actors who needed to get "in the mood," these three instinctive cut-ups were able to kid on the sidelines one second and jump up and do the scene to perfection the next, unsettling the director who was used to more introspection from his casts. Often there were dirty stories and they would catch Judy trying to eavesdrop. The boys would joke with her and tell her to get lost.

"What I remember most about Judy is how she used to love to laugh," commented Haley recently. "She was full of laughter. And pep. She didn't need pills, but the poor sucker got hooked on them. Not while she was on *Oz*. The pills started when she turned out pictures faster than Metro could make money on them."

Nevertheless, showing a desire for the privacy she would demand on more troubled future occasions, Judy often would retire alone or with a friend or two to her own new "star treatment" yellow trailer, replete with make-up room and bathroom. She did not mix with the company as much as on previous pictures. When she was absent from the set for a week with a cold, it cost the studio $150,000. She would cost MGM much, much more as the years wore on, and when her habitual tardiness and absenteeism through her peak forties period were later made known, it seemed a miracle that her many films not only turned out so well but that they ever got made in the first place. Some people couldn't help wondering how, and why, MGM put up with her maddeningly erratic behavior. Perhaps the moguls liked her, felt responsible for her (her

110

A close view of Bert Lahr's Lion make-up

The Tin Woodman bemoans his fate in
Jack Haley's "breathless, thin falsetto."

most frequent producer, Arthur Freed, had only kind things to say about her right up to his death in 1973); perhaps, too, as Haley suggested, they liked her films' grosses.

Much later, Judy accused MGM of getting her on pills—pills to put her to sleep after long, keyed-up days at the studios, pills to wake her up and keep her going for the next day's work. Skeptics have pointed out that Mayer, almost fanatic in his moralistic personal attitudes, would never have permitted regular drug-taking as part of the MGM regimen but would have fired anyone he caught inflicting it on any member of his "family" of stars.

It was known that the increasingly unstable Judy came to embroider her anecdotes for effect. One of her favorite stories, which she even told on television, was how those three veterans, Bolger, Haley and Lahr, would upstage her on the Yellow Brick Road, pushing her to the rear as they marched along. "And Mr. Fleming, a darling man who was always on a boom, would yell, 'You three dirty hams, let the little girl in there!' " was how Judy ended her recollection.

The three men have denied this. "We were bigger than she was, that's all," Bolger told *TV Guide*. "Besides, we were all trying to do our parts. I was constantly falling, Lahr had that tail to handle [most of the time it was worked by a stagehand, who stood on a catwalk and maneuvered the tail with a fishing pole] and Haley just clogged along. Who had *time* to upstage anybody?"

Haley is even more pointed: "After a while, I guess, she just started to believe it . . . How could [that story] be? When we go off to see the Wizard we're locked arm in arm, and every shot is a long shot. How can you push someone out of the picture with a long shot?"

Bolger noted that there was a lengthy shooting schedule, and "we became almost a family." He sometimes helped Judy with her homework during lulls.

Legitimate scene-stealing occurred, as happens on many films; but certainly Lahr, Haley and Bolger had their hands full just surviving under the hot lights in their cumbersome make-up, which was devised by Jack Dawn during six months of experimentation. It was heavy on sponge rubber applied to the face and then colored to match—even the Witch's chin and nose were augmented with this substance. The principals in character make-up got up at five A.M. to be in the Make-up Department at seven. Jack Dawn gave each player a make-up man apiece, and they spent two hours each day in the application, seeing to it that the make-up did not obscure the distinctive, all-important facial characteristics of the actors. The sponge rubber on Lahr's upper lip prevented him from eating regular lunches; while in Lion costume he had to sip his meals through a straw.

"Bert couldn't eat with that straw, but somehow he ate more than any of us," Bolger remarked. "One day he asked me, 'What should I do? I'm starving!' 'Bert,' I said, 'just float around on your gas'." (Bolger learned to dish it out, too.)

The three actors looked so grotesque MGM wouldn't allow them to eat in the commissary. They were given a bungalow.

Haley recalls, "It was abominably tough. The best time was when the teacher who had to be on the set all the time to give Judy her lessons would holler: 'Judy! It's time for school.' That meant we could take that make-up off."

Lahr's Lion suit, which it took the wardrobe department two months to make from real lion skins, weighed fifty pounds. Bolger's Scarecrow face was covered with transparent burlap which was glued on and then painted. Haley, unable to sit in his "tin union suit," as he called it, was "dog tired" all the time from moonlighting on a radio series and often dozed between calls on a leaning board specially designed for him. Lahr, a button-twisting,

A happy Judy Garland, with Toto

chronic worrier, couldn't get over this. "That Haley could sleep on a meathook," he cracked.

Then there were the voices for the three peculiar Oz residents. The slightly hoarse, low, gulping voice for the Scarecrow came easily to Ray Bolger, and Bert Lahr's own inimitable slangy speech was indivisible from his Cowardly Lion. There was more concern over how Jack Haley's Tin Woodman should talk. Fleming and Haley tossed ideas around for a while until Haley came up with the eminently usable notion of speaking with the same breathless, thin falsetto he affected when he told his four-year-old grandson bedtime stories.

Fleming had a shrewd ploy to keep his more heavily costumed and made-up principals interested during the delays. When he saw them beginning to wilt, he would call a huddle, tell them he was having trouble with the next scene and ask their advice. He treated Judy tenderly, calling her "Judalein" throughout the shooting. (Her sister Jimmy, who had just given birth to the young actress' only niece and named her Judy, liked Fleming's nickname—which means "little Judy" in German—so much she re-named the infant Judalein.)

Judy was the only one who never seemed dispirited. Bolger thought her "a dumpy little kid" when she first walked on the set, but "when the kleig lights shone on her she was marked by a total lack of inhibition and an amazing intensity." Margaret Hamilton had a couple of long talks with her then, and remembers that Judy, like any other teenager, was excited about being graduated from high school that June. "Isn't it wonderful, I'm going to graduate with a class!" Judy exclaimed, adding that it was "almost the first thing" she'd done that "every other girl does." She proudly fetched the demure white dress she had bought for the event to show Miss Hamilton. "Then, around graduation time,

there was some talk of sending her on a tour to promote the movie," Miss Hamilton said. "I don't know if she ever got to wear her dress."

A few years ago, Miss Hamilton discussed *The Wizard of Oz* with *The New York Times'* Howard Thompson on the occasion of its imminent thirteenth telecast. "I adore the picture," the gentle, far-from-boisterous, real-life Margaret Hamilton admitted. "Last year I was doing repertory in Seattle, where I saw it on a big color set in the home of friends. And that ending always gets to me, that last line—'there's no place like home.' Especially since poor Judy, with her insecurities, never really reached home."

As *The Wizard of Oz* was nearing completion, *Gone with the Wind* began shooting at the Selznick Studio (and sometimes at MGM, which was releasing it), with George Cukor directing. But it just wasn't Cukor's season. After two-and-a-half weeks, producer David Selznick fired the distinguished director who had also left *Wizard*. Indispensable leading man Clark Gable complained that Cukor had been spending too much time coaching leading ladies Vivien Leigh and Olivia de Havilland. In addition, Cukor was working too slowly (Gable had to finish the picture by a certain date) and the ubiquitous Selznick wanted more emphasis on his epic's spectacle than character-motivated Cukor was providing. Gable suggested that his pal Victor Fleming replace Cukor—just as Fleming had on *Wizard*! Selznick, however, was interested in King Vidor, director of such pictures as *The Champ* (1931), with child star Jackie Cooper.

Approached, Vidor spent the week-end reading the *Gone with the Wind* script, but decided against doing such a gigantic film without preparation. Then he was asked if he would take over the last scenes for *Wizard of Oz* if Victor Fleming took on *Gone with the Wind*, to which he agreed. Fleming— Margaret Hamilton says she didn't believe he

had a contract, so he could leave anytime —showed him around the sets and briefed him, exiting the production that same night. Vidor worked about three weeks on it, wrapping up the picture after having shot Judy's "Over the Rainbow" number, among other, mostly non-Technicolor scenes.

"I always wanted to do a musical film," Vidor says. "I wanted to keep the movement going, just as we had in silent pictures. And I was able to do that in that film [in] my contribution to it. I also did some of the cyclone scenes, and 'We're Off to See the Wizard'—working with Bert Lahr, Ray Bolger, Jack Haley and Judy Garland."

He refused credit, and as long as Fleming lived (he died in 1949) Vidor never mentioned that he had directed Judy Garland's most famous screen song. Vidor never got another chance to work with a musical.

Victor Fleming was not out of the picture yet, however. When *Wizard of Oz* finished principal photography on March 16, 1939, six months after it had started, Fleming, who was still helming *Gone with the Wind* by day, raced from the nearby Selznick Studio to MGM's cutting rooms where night after night he helped film editor Blanche Sewell on *Wizard*. This work on *Wizard*, heightened by the troubles experienced in directing the Selznick production, eventually caused him to miss two weeks of *Wind* shooting, claiming a "nervous breakdown."

Fleming probably thought it was worth it, though. Even the most dedicated film buff would be hard put to think of another instance when one director worked simultaneously on two such classic, beloved movies that together have made so many of the ten-best-films-of-all-time lists.

117

Dorothy is greeted by the Lollipop Guild.

The Music 5

Few movie musicals—or stage or television musicals, for that matter—have had songs as well integrated as those in *The Wizard of Oz*. They flow so naturally out of the action that the viewer sometimes doesn't even realize he's been sung to, until he leaves (these days) the living room, humming the tunes.

Incredibly, the whole score was written in only two months.

The Depression had brought Harold Arlen, composer, and E. Y. ("Yip") Harburg, lyricist, to Hollywood, as it had many other theater-oriented songwriters of even greater renown who wanted to work. Arlen has said, "There were plenty of other major songwriters who were damned unhappy and shocked when they heard we'd gotten it [*The Wizard of Oz*], because they'd all been sitting around *waiting* for that job." Besides Arlen and Harburg, who were always in contention, others mentioned early for the assignment were lyricists Dorothy Fields and Ira Gershwin and composers Nacio Herb Brown and Jerome Kern. Associate producer Arthur Freed, by virtue of his own songwriting expertise, was given the responsibility for all important musical matters and had talked with his close friend, the illustrious Kern, who was interested in writing the score. But after seeing their

Broadway musical *Hooray for What?*, an antiwar satire directed by Vincente Minnelli (who would be Judy Garland's second husband), and hearing the show's song "In the Shade of the New Apple Tree," Freed decided on Arlen and Harburg. " 'New Apple Tree' got us *Wizard of Oz*," noted Arlen.

In that tune, Freed heard "all the sparkle and lightness he hoped could be put into the score of the new film," wrote Edward Jablonski in his biography of Arlen, *Happy with the Blues*. "Freed used the song as an arguing point when he brought up the names of Arlen and Harburg . . . Harburg, Freed felt, had a wonderful feeling for fantasy that, coupled with Arlen's musical fancy, might produce the right songs for the contemplated filming . . . Freed made his point." In July, 1938, *The Hollywood Reporter* announced that Harold Arlen and E.Y. Harburg had been signed to write the songs for MGM's most ambitious musical.

Filming was to begin in September, 1938.

Arlen and Harburg took houses a block apart in Beverly Hills, not far from Judy, and set to work, also helping touch up the screenplay here and there so that the characters and their songs would mesh better. They did not want the usual plot-halting "number" insertions.

Lyricist E. Y. ("Yip") Harburg today

Harburg apprised in Max Wilk's *They're Playing Our Song*: "It was a chance to express ourselves in terms we'd never been offered before. I loved the idea of having the freedom to do lyrics that were not just songs but *scenes*. That was our own idea, to take some of the book and do some of the scenes in complete verse, such as the scenes in Munchkinland. It gave me wider scope. Not just 32-bar songs, but what would amount to

the acting out of entire scenes, dialogue in verse and set to Harold's modern music. All of that had to be thought out by us and then brought in and shown to the director so he could see what we were getting at. Things like the three Lullabye girls, and the three tough kids who represented the Lollipop Guild. And the Coroner, who came to avow that the Witch was 'dead, most sincerely dead.' " All this was dreamed up by the two tunesmiths, as was the

Composer Harold Arlen today

theme of "Over the Rainbow" since no rainbow was mentioned in the L. Frank Baum book.

"Over the Rainbow," Judy's seismically affecting trademark song, was written at the eleventh hour. The writers had composed the lighter tunes (or "lemon drop songs," as they like to call them) when Freed requested a ballad to balance things, as well as to effect the transition from Kansas to Oz. The melody just came to Arlen one evening in front of Schwab's legendary drugstore on Sunset Boulevard while he and his wife were driving to Grauman's Chinese Theatre. He jotted it down in the car. One aspect in its creation was to give him a little trouble: the melody of the central line of the song's bridge ("Someday I'll wish upon a star . . ."). "Harold," advised Harburg, "you know that whistle you use when you call your dog into the house? Try that." Arlen did, and the bridge to the "Rainbow" was found.

Difficulties with the song were really just beginning. For one thing, Harburg at first thought the melody too powerful for a little farm girl to sing, a composition better suited to a Nelson Eddy. "Harold struck a brave and inspired symphonic theme. It is not a little child's nursery song. It's a great big theme that you could easily build a symphony around . . . we brought it down with those colorful and child-like words," explained Harburg.

Everyone met at Arlen's house for the debut of the number. Arthur Freed, Roger Edens and sixteen-year-old Judy were there, and Arlen played his music on the piano while Harburg recited the lyrics. Then Judy tried it. She loved the song immediately, showing an uncanny, even weird ability (in view of its later significance in her life) to understand and render the piece on one listen, even though she did not read music. All agreed it was a winner.

The first sneak preview of *The Wizard of Oz*, recalls producer Mervyn LeRoy, was held in San Bernardino, where the audience response was "terrific." Then, during the usual lobby conference afterward, one MGM producer opined that the song "Over the Rainbow" slowed the picture down and should be cut. Other studio executives—an insecure breed too often motivated by fear, according to LeRoy—agreed in a chain reaction and a furor started that was not to be resolved for some time.

"All the other songs were in a faster, catchier tempo. They were the sort of melodies the public could latch on to quickly," LeRoy expanded. " 'Over the Rainbow,' on the other hand, was a ballad, and it always takes a private ear several hearings before it appreciates a ballad . . . I knew in my heart that 'Over the Rainbow' would be a hit, but I had had the benefit of hearing it often. I

tried to persuade them that the song was a good one, but I seemed to be arguing in vain."

Studio boss Louis B. Mayer, who would make the final decision, listened intently to both factions. Opponents included Sam Katz, executive producer of the musical division, who thought the whole score "above the heads of children," and music publisher Jack Robbins, who thought "Over the Rainbow" sounded "like a child's piano exercise. Nobody will sing it—who'll buy the sheet music?"

Arthur Freed was the song's most vociferous champion. The picture was previewed several times without this number; on each occasion he stormed into Mayer's office to protest.

Arlen and Harburg were crestfallen, powerless. After a while Arlen vowed to his wife, "No more previews. From now on I'm just going to write the best I can, turn 'em in and forget 'em."

Many years and much heartbreak later, Judy said she wasn't aware until the first preview that they were mulling cutting "Over the Rainbow." She couldn't understand it "because it was such a beautiful song. However, in those days I had very little to say about anything. As for my feelings towards 'Over the Rainbow' now, it has become part of my life. It is so symbolic of everybody's dream and wish that I am sure that's why people sometimes get tears in their eyes when they hear it. I have sung it dozens of times and it is still the song that is closest to my heart."

Mel Tormé backed her up—for practically the only time—in his memoir of their television association, *The Other Side of the Rainbow: With Judy Garland on the Dawn Patrol*: "We suggested doing a rather funny bit built around 'Over the Rainbow' . . . 'There will be *no* jokes of any kind about 'Over the Rainbow'!' she said evenly. 'It's kind of . . . sacred. I don't want anybody *anywhere* to lose the thing they have about Dorothy or that song!' "

Arthur Freed, associate producer of *The Wizard of Oz*

(Judy was nothing if not mercurial. When, after a command performance in England, the Queen Mother told Judy her singing of "Over the Rainbow" never failed to bring a lump to her throat, Judy was alleged to have replied, "Ma'am, that song has plagued me all my life. You know, it's hard to be remembered by a song you first sang thirty years ago. It's like being a grandmother in pigtails.")

Finally, Freed gave Mayer an ultimatum: "The song stays—or I go!" Mayer had always respected his friend's taste; he had big plans for him at the studio.

"Over the Rainbow" was saved (although even today one notices that the scene comes on with a sudden, almost jerky, re-inserted look) and went on to win the Academy Award for Best Song that year. As did Herbert Stothart for his Original Score (musical adaptation) which combined original material with fragments from such classical composers as Schumann, Mendelssohn and Moussorgsky, one haunting bit being the chant "The March of the Winkies" which resembled "The Song of the Volga Boatman" but is credited to Stothart and Roger Edens.*

Not so lucky was "The Jitterbug."

One of the most complicated numbers, as well as scenes, "The Jitterbug" took five weeks to get on film (the shooting time for many entire pictures) and featured Judy Garland, Bert Lahr, Ray Bolger, Jack Haley and assorted dancing trees and flowers. "*Everything* danced," says lyricist Harburg. It was perhaps inspired by news coverage of hundreds and thousands of frenzied teen-agers jitterbugging to the new "swing" music

in theater aisles and around bandstands across the nation. The *Wizard of Oz* "Jitterbug" was deleted at the suggestion, this time, of Freed himself, who after viewing the finished production for the first time told director Victor Fleming, "I think you should cut out that whole scene where the Jitterbug bites Bert Lahr and they do the 'Jitterbug Dance' with Judy singing. It slows the picture down and is irrelevant to the story." The film's original two-hour running time was deemed too long to hold the interest of youngsters—it eventually was trimmed to a hundred minutes for release. Fleming insisted "The Jitterbug" remain for the first preview, but it was removed without incident (then) for all subsequent showings; although Judy did sing it on her separately recorded Decca album of the movie's tunes (this was in pre-sound track LP days) and in 1963 she resurrected the ditty with guest star Ray Bolger on her short-lived television show, where it was one of the series' highlights. (For Judy's show, CBS built a Yellow Brick Road from her dressing room to the stage.)

Actually, the number was not "irrelevant" to the story, nor was the production's length the only reason that has been given for its omission.

" 'The Jitterbug' was sung in the film by all four principals in a segment of which there are still traces," confirms Miles Kreuger, popular music historian. "When they journey into the Haunted Forest, the camera pulls back to reveal the Witch and a Winged Monkey observing them in the crystal ball. The Witch runs to the window and cries to the flotilla of Winged Monkeys flying by that she wants them to bring back that little girl and her dog, too. Meanwhile, she will send a little insect ahead that will take the fight out of them. In today's prints, this reference is wholly unexplained, for the next shot, which of course follows the cut number, shows the Monkeys swooping down on the quartet and carrying off Dorothy and Toto."

*The other 1939 Best Song contenders: "Faithful Forever," by Ralph Rainger and Leo Robin, from *Gulliver's Travels*; "I Poured My Heart into a Song," by Irving Berlin, from *Second Fiddle*; and "Wishing," by Buddy DeSylva, from *Love Affair*. Stothart's competition included no less than eleven other scores. Among them: *Gone with the Wind*, by Max Steiner; *Of Mice and Men*, by Aaron Copland; and *Wuthering Heights*, by Alfred Newman.

Herbert Stothart at work on his original score for the film

The Winkies — the Witch's guards

"Originally," Kreuger continues, "the number was not unlike the ballet of *The Red Shoes* in that the bug's syncopated eyes made them all dance until they were too exhausted to fight off the Monkeys. As Harold Arlen, E.Y. Harburg and Ken Darby [one of the picture's arrangers] have all explained, it was felt upon completion of the film that a classic had been produced and jitterbugging would date the picture in just a few years."

The Jitterbug as a popular dance lasted for decades, though, and today the number's appearance in *The Wizard of Oz* would give it an added fillip of nostalgia. In description, it certainly did not sound like a musical interlude to slow down a movie, with its wild staging and alliterative, tongue-twisting lyrics: "Oh! The bees in the breeze and the bats in the trees have a terrible, horrible buzz/But the bees in the breeze and the bats in the trees couldn't do what the Jitterbug does," etc.

The masses now caught up in Garland worship, as well as those who simply admire the film, bemoan the loss of this exciting-sounding musical phantasmagoria. (Margaret Hamilton recalls it as "great.") The cutting, furthermore, left the last quarter of the picture comparatively without music, damaging the rhythm of the film.

Yet another possible reason for the exclusion has been that Bert Lahr, who just about stole the movie anyway, was so strong in this number that he eclipsed his partners, including Judy, whom MGM (and Freed) was pushing for stardom. Without "The Jitterbug," some have said, Lahr's grip on the picture was lessened to Judy's benefit.

The final significant musical cut was the "Renovation Sequence," which had come last on the program. It depicted the celebration of Emerald City residents when Dorothy and friends returned over a dissolving "rainbow bridge" (a tricky bit of special effects magic also lost to viewers on the cutting room floor)

to the Wizard with proof that the Wicked Witch of the West was dead.

Lyricist Harburg does feel that *The Wizard of Oz* was indeed "mangled" by the hierarchy after completion, adding, nevertheless, that he and Arlen are still grateful and not a little incredulous that so much of their material did survive big studio machinations and make it into the release prints.

Considerable unbilled performing talent was employed in the musical portions of *The Wizard of Oz*—portions which Metro, incidentally, first wanted Busby Berkeley to stage; Bobby Connolly finally was credited with them. (Later that year, Berkeley came over from Warner Brothers to direct the entire *Babes in Arms*, Arthur Freed's first title as a full-fledged movie producer.)

Lorraine Bridges dubbed Billie Burke's singing voice on "Munchkinland (Come Out, Come Out, Wherever You Are)", while Adriana Caselotti—whose most famous job remains the singing and speaking voice for Snow White in Walt Disney's *Snow White and the Seven Dwarfs* (1938)—was the off-screen soprano heard briefly during Jack Haley's "If I Only Had a Heart." The Rhythmettes vocalized on several parts of the sound track, including the numbers "Munchkinland" (over the opening credits and upon Dorothy's arrival in Oz), a reprise of "Over the Rainbow", and "Optimistic Voices." (While it never became as well-known as some of the others, the latter is a jubilant little song which—despite its casual title and the fact that Herbert Stothart is listed as co-composer of its music—was especially liked by Arlen and Harburg, as it heralds not only the four principals' escape from the woods and an evil spell but, on another level, the end of the Depression.) A popular girl trio called the Three Debutantes provided the voices of the toe-dancing Lullabye League, and John Dodson, Rad

Two views of the "Renovation Sequence," cut from the film

Dorothy frees the Winkies.

Robinson and Bud Linn, who with MGM's Ken Darby earlier had formed the singing quartet known as the King's Men, were the voices of the three Lollipop Guild toughs. Robinson and Linn were the voices, too, of the Munchkin Coroner and District Attorney (who wanted "to verify it legally"), and Darby himself sang the role of the Mayor of the Munchkin City. The St. Joseph Choir was heard in the Munchkinland sequence.

In *High Fidelity* Magazine, Miles Kreuger recently wrote: "At the time, all film recording was made optically, using cameras that ran at a standard speed of ninety feet a minute. In order to speed up the Munchkin voices, it was necessary to slow down the recording camera. This was accomplished by the director of MGM's sound department, Douglas Shearer, who ground special gears to slow down the recording camera to proper speed. Only deep voices were used for the male characters, as tenors would have sounded too squeaky when sped up. Similarly, the Winkies, who guard the Witch's castle, were recorded faster than is natural to sound, very ominous and deep-voiced, and tenors were used for this group."

Judy Garland recorded the Decca Records album of *Wizard of Oz* songs soon after the film was released, backed by Victor Young and his Orchestra, the Ken Darby Singers and Cliff Edwards. It took seventeen years, however, for MGM—spurred by the movie's success on television—to issue the twelve-inch sound track album LP, replete with dialogue extracts that helped to tell the story. Missing from the LP were the "Jitterbug" and "Merry Old Land of Oz" numbers, which *were* included on the early Decca four-record 78-rpm album set.

The Wizard of Oz, with the movie's score, has become something of a stock-theater staple. Margaret Hamilton judges that she has done it about ten times, most recently during the summer of 1975 in St. Louis and Kansas City, Missouri. This unlikely version starred the Hudson Brothers of television, nightclubs and recordings as the Scarecrow, the Tin Woodman and the Cowardly Lion, with Karen Wyman as Dorothy. It contained "smidgens of bathroom humor" that did not please Miss Hamilton. "But then, they're always adding new things to these stock productions. I remember another time when little Dorothy suddenly broke into singing 'Someday My Prince Will Come,' which of course is from *Snow White*!"

Legends have sprung up over the years about several of the Arlen-Harburg *Wizard* songs.

One of the most persistent has been that "We're Off to See the Wizard" was adopted as a theme song by the Australians during World War II. However, a Wallaroo, Australia, letter-writer to *Films in Review* in 1958 debunked this story: "According to the official history, during the 1941 battle for Bardia, some Australian soldiers advanced upon the Italian lines singing 'South of the Border,' which was then popular. Later, some British war correspondents arrived in the area and were told by a Captain P. Woodhill that some of the soldiers had sung as they advanced. When asked what they had sung, Woodhill, being weary and of a puckish humor, replied, 'The Wizard of Oz.' And so was born another legend."

Unsquelched is the legend attached to the firing during production of an MGM employee of indeterminate station. After listening to the Munchkins trill "Ding-dong! The Witch is dead!/Which old witch? The Wicked Witch" all day, this unfortunate man took to singing it while he worked, too; but the words kept coming out "Ding-dong! The Bitch is dead/Which old bitch? The Wicked Bitch." Leo the Lion did not roar with laughter.

The Legend 6

The east and west coast openings of *The Wizard of Oz*, with their accompanying excitement, are still recalled more vividly by witnesses than are most motion pictures.

The night before *Wizard* had its New York debut at the Capitol Theater on the scorching hot day of August 17, 1939, ticket-buyers of all ages began lining up outside the movie palace. When the theater—which seated 5,400—opened in the morning, police estimated that there were 4,000 waiting to get in. The theater's press agent counted 20,000. Everyone agreed that New York probably had never seen a queue that long for a "picture show"—it virtually encircled the block.

Of course, there was an "extra added attraction" in this particular case. The film's leading lady, Judy Garland, and her frequent partner, the immensely popular Mickey Rooney, had been set to appear for the first week of the run, performing five times each day between showings of the film (of which, incidentally, MGM had prepared a record number of five hundred and fifty prints). And this the youngsters did, to tumultuous audience acclaim—Judy singing and clowning with Mickey, who also did impressions and played the drums with the band of George (Georgie) Stoll (associate conductor on *Wizard*). Thirty-seven thousand cash customers were clocked on opening day, the mobs kept in check by sixty policemen. Once during the week Judy, exhausted, fainted backstage just before she was to go on, but recovered in time to join Rooney, ever the trouper, who was on stage vamping. In those days, when film stars were gods and goddesses kept remote from the public by their studios, it was very unusual for movie players of their stature to be so visible in person. The Capitol booking was a testament to the vast appeal of Rooney and Garland.

Two nights before the New York opening, *The Wizard of Oz* was unveiled at Hollywood's Grauman's Chinese Theatre in what is still alluded to as a quintessential movieland premiere right out of Nathanael West's *The Day of the Locust*. Publicity people judged the throng jamming Hollywood Boulevard at 12,000. A reported six thousand sat from four P.M.—five hours before the picture started—until nearly midnight in special stands erected on the curb. Thousands more milled in the street and the theater's spacious forecourt, where minute "Munchkins" from the film frolicked on a Yellow Brick Road surrounded by waving cornstalks transplanted from the movie set. Author L. Frank Baum's widow attended, as did Fred Stone, star of the early-century stage

presentation. Mounted police patroled the area.

Only once on either coast did the Ozmania get out of hand. That was in Hollywood when Hedy Lamarr, MGM's newest glamour girl, stepped out of her limousine in front of Grauman's and was almost crushed by fans.

The Wizard of Oz was nominated by the Motion Picture Academy of Arts and Sciences as the Best Picture of 1939, losing to perhaps

the one film about which there could be no grumbling: *Gone with the Wind*.

The reviews were generally favorable. "*The Wizard of Oz* should settle an old Hollywood controversy: whether fantasy can be presented on the screen as successfully with human actors as with cartoons. It can," nodded *Time* Magazine, adding, "It floats in the same rare atmosphere of enchantment that distinguished Walt Disney's *Snow White and*

the *Seven Dwarfs*." Frank Nugent, writing in *The New York Times*, called it "A delightful piece of wonder-working . . . Judy Garland's Dorothy is a pert and fresh-faced miss with the wonder-lit eyes of a believer in fairy tales." *The New York Daily News'* Kate Cameron gave the film four stars, the paper's highest rating, recognizing Judy Garland to be "as clever a little actress as she is a singer"; while *Variety* saluted the film as "a pushover

for the children and family biz." *The New York Post's* Archer Winsten chorused: "A beautiful and humorous fantasy, the appeal of which is not limited to children . . . [It's] a picture to put on your things-to-do today list . . . The performances are beyond cavil."

The consensus was that Bert Lahr "romps off with the acting honors," as Rose Pelswick reported in *The New York Journal-American*. "The Lahr roar, with just the proper note of

difference in it," continued Frank Nugent, "is one of the laughingest sounds the screen has uttered since the talkies came in." A writer archly known as "Beverly Hills," reviewing for *Liberty* Magazine, found "Lahr's Lion a richly amusing creation, right after Androcles' own heart." In *The New York World-Telegram*, William Boehnel wrote, "Most of the players are excellent, but standing out above all the others is Bert Lahr, who somehow gives the film just the fillip it needs."

Fault-finders were scarce. Among them were William Boehnel and, in *The New Republic*, Otis Ferguson. Both filed similar complaints about the production, although the degree of their overall disapproval varied greatly. The more equivocating Boehnel, for instance, thought it "a handsomely mounted, frequently delightful and charming fantasy which cries out for the light, deft, humorous touch of a Walt Disney. This may sound like carping criticism of a film which has more than a generous share of fun in it, but the fact remains that much of the charm which is inherent in this engaging fairy tale is lost because of heavy-handed treatment." Ferguson was nasty and startlingly anti-Judy, barking that *The Wizard of Oz* tried to emulate *Snow White*, elucidating that "[The film] has dwarfs, music, Technicolor, freak characters and Judy Garland. It can't be expected to have a sense of humor as well—and as for the light touch of fantasy, it weighs like a pound of fruitcake soaking wet . . . [Frank] Morgan is the only unaffected trouper in the bunch; the rest either try too hard or are Judy Garland. It isn't that this little slip of a miss spoils the fantasy so much as that her thumping, overgrown gambols are characteristic of its treatment here: when she is merry the house shakes, and everybody gets wet when she is lorn."

Astonishingly, the Arlen-Harburg songs came in for some brickbats, too. Frank

Judy Garland in
the Lux Radio
Theatre version
of the film,
December, 1950

Nugent, of all cinema savants, opined, "The only serious objection we might entertain is that the score, with the exception of the Lahr songs, is neither as zestful nor as tuneful as the occasion warranted." An oddly contradictory critique was rendered by *Liberty*'s Beverly Hills: "Music enlivens every foot of the film and there are some mildly tinkling tunes." ("Howzzat?," Bert Lahr might have remarked after reading the latter.)

Such negative reactions were in the vast minority in 1939, and today they would be practically sacrilegious.

In films, when a certain formula clicks (as, say, MGM's Hardy family did), it is more than likely—even today—that Hollywood will repeat itself quickly. Therefore, considering the magnitude of the success of *The Wizard of Oz*, it is surprising to realize that few of its extraordinarily congruent participants ever worked with Judy Garland again on the screen. Associate producer Arthur Freed was the notable exception: he produced the majority of Judy's hits within his elite Freed Unit at Metro. But she never again performed under the aegis of her *Wizard* producer, Mervyn LeRoy, who went back to directing such "prestige" films as *Waterloo Bridge* (1940), *Random Harvest* (1942) and *Little Women* (1949); or with her director, the late Victor Fleming, whose last film was *Joan of Arc* (1948), starring Ingrid Bergman. Margaret Hamilton supported Judy in her next, *Babes in Arms* (1939), and Ray Bolger was with her again in *The Harvey Girls* (1946)—their final film associations with the younger player. Judy, Bert Lahr, Jack Haley and Frank Morgan did no further pictures together, although Morgan and Judy were among the many guest names in the all-star *Thousands Cheer* (1943). (In 1949, Morgan had started

Top to bottom: Tiger Haynes, Ted Ross, Stephanie Mills, and Hinton Battle in the Broadway production of THE WIZ

141

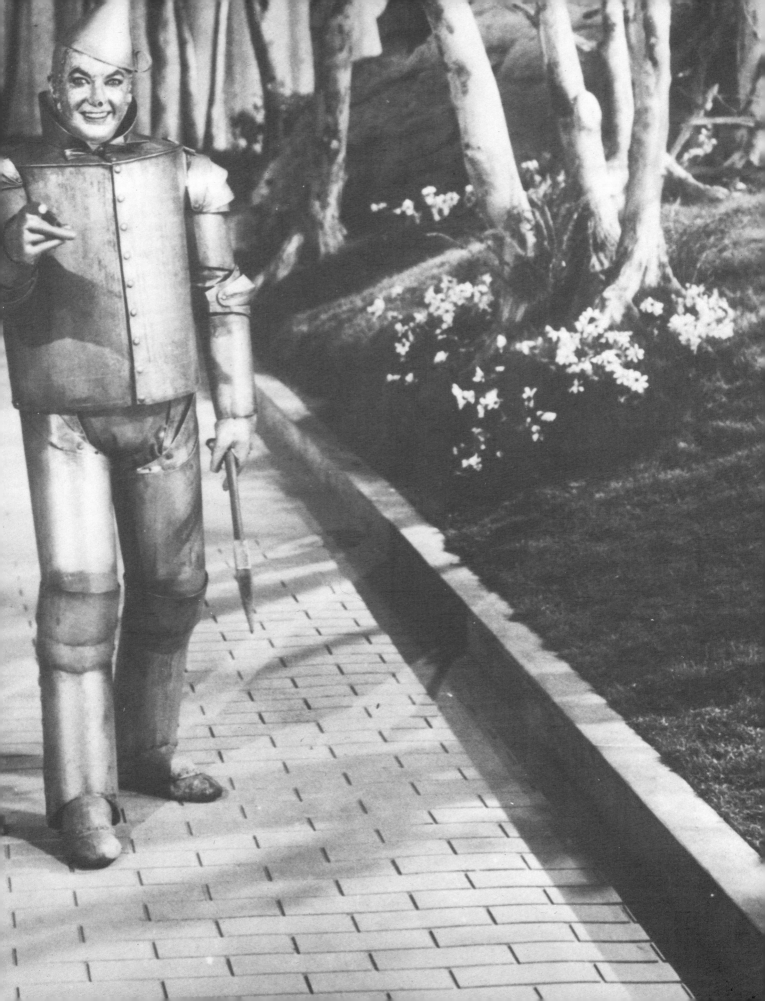

Annie Get Your Gun with Judy when a fatal heart attack caused him to be replaced by Louis Calhern and a "nervous breakdown" caused Judy to be replaced by Betty Hutton.) Neither Clara Blandick nor Charley Grapewin graced any more Garland movies.

Even songwriters Arlen and Harburg only did one other entire Garland film score together, and that during the actress' declining years: the Warner Brothers cartoon feature *Gay Purr-ee* (1962). The following year they produced the title tune for Judy's last picture, United Artists' *I Could Go on Singing*. Arlen, however, together with lyricist Ira Gershwin, did compose the songs for her last good vehicle, Warners' *A Star is Born* (1954), but unfortunately some of their best tunes were cut from general release prints in a notorious example of studio-engineered film butchering.

There was no *The Wizard of Oz II*. MGM pondered a sequel briefly in the early forties, but nothing came of it. (*The Wizard of Oz* was reissued in the late forties and, as *Variety* put it, did "boff biz" all over again.) Aside from Judy's *Lux Radio Theatre* repeat of her *Wizard* role in December, 1950, it was decades before Frank Baum's Oz characters were importantly revived. Filmation Associates' animated feature *Journey Back to Oz* (1962) exploitatively related the further adventures of Dorothy and her companions, with Liza Minnelli replacing her mother, Judy Garland, on the sound track. At sixteen and just starting out in show business, Liza was the same age as Judy when she had played the Kansas farm girl. Milton Berle was the voice of the Cowardly Lion; Mickey Rooney, the Scarecrow; Margaret Hamilton, Auntie Em this time; and Ethel Merman was the Wicked Witch. Sammy Cahn and Jimmy Van Heusen wrote the score. The film's release was held up until the seventies, when it was not well-received. In 1975, however, Baum's original Oz tale was given one of its most successful,

timely dramatizations in the all-black Broadway musical version titled *The Wiz*, with a book by William F. Brown and music and lyrics by Charlie Smalls. Young Stephanie Mills played Dorothy. It won seven of the theater's Tony Awards, including Best Musical.

The popularity of the movie is unabating.

A smaller-scale Disneyland-type Wizardland was erected on a North Carolina mountaintop some years ago, with Ray Bolger as the guiding force behind the enterprise. Bolger revealed plans to expand the concept to other, larger locations, but they do not appear to have been realized.

In recent months alone, there have been a new line of *Wizard of Oz* dolls; a hit record by Elton John, titled "Goodbye, Yellow Brick Road"; Scarecrow and Tin Woodman pitched product commercials on TV; children's clothing stores called The Wizard of Oz; and a deluxe comic book series designed after the film. There are even tiny doughnuts called Munchkins. Furthermore, a number of *Wizard of Oz* scenes were featured in the surprise hit film of 1974, *That's Entertainment!*, a compilation of clips from nearly fifty years of MGM musicals. The film was produced, directed and written by Jack Haley, Jr.—who was to marry Judy's now superstar daughter, Liza.

The Wizard of Oz, then, had been a highly successful movie and was fondly recalled; but, ironically, it was television—the big screen's great nemesis—that brought *The Wizard* recognition as a masterwork of the cinema. *And* the status of an institution.

In 1956, it became one of the first features from MGM's vast, glossy library to reach television when the studio leased it to CBS, which paid $225,000 per showing under a contract with MGM that committed the network to two telecastings of the film plus an option on two more. Mervyn LeRoy remembers that

1060-141

CBS, with a respect and trepidation that would soon become uncharacteristic, asked the producer to cut five minutes from the movie for TV. He found this impossible, managing only one minute. The network acquiesced. The first showing was that fall on a Saturday evening from nine to eleven, sponsored by Ford. Don Miller, writing in *Films in Review* then, noted "that Trendex [poll-takers] claimed the other things on TV that night, including Sid Caesar, Lawrence Welk, George Gobel and *Masquerade Party*, had but half or a third of the audience *Wizard* did . . . A year ago a neighborhood theater could rent *Wizard of Oz* for $15 or so, and not do too much business."

Television changed all that.

CBS' first repeat occurred in 1959, and John Crosby in *The New York Herald-Tribune* raved, "Television—any television—looks awfully prosaic, awfully ordinary after *Wizard of Oz*. It is pure magic." CBS eventually renewed its original contract with MGM. In 1967, the movie company—by then in financial straits—signed a more lucrative new five-year deal with NBC, which agreed to pay MGM $800,000 per annual showing, nearly four times as much as CBS had been paying.

After the 1975 NBC telecast of *Wizard of Oz*, it was announced that CBS had reacquired the picture as an annual special under a five-year contract, effective with the 1976 showing. CBS was believed to be paying MGM $4,000,000 for the five contracted airings. The Hollywood movie studio already had been in receipt of a total of $7,600,000 for renting out the film to television.

The Wizard of Oz is the only movie presented by network television as a prime time event year after year. At this writing late in 1975, it has appeared on home screens seventeen times, usually during the Easter season and early in the evening so that youngsters can watch. It always clobbers the competition.

"In 1965 an interesting rating system was noticed in Toronto," wrote Al DiOrio, Jr., in his biography of Judy Garland, *Little Girl Lost*. "It seems that the home-viewers watching the movie were so enthralled by it that they wouldn't leave their seats for anything. As soon as the movie was over, however, the water department reported a simultaneous flushing of millions of toilets in the area!"

Margaret Hamilton told Robert C. Roman in *After Dark* Magazine that the picture keeps coming back every year "because it's such a beautiful film. I don't think any of us knew how lovely it was at first. But, after a while, we all began to feel it coming together—and we knew we had something. I can watch it again and again and remember wonderful Judy, Bert, Ray, Jack, Billie, Frank and how wonderful they all were. The scene that always gets to me, though, and I think it's one of the most appealing scenes I've ever seen, is the one where the Wizard gives the gifts to them at the end. Frank was just like that as a person. And every time I see him do it, the tears come to my eyes. I listen to the words. I think of Frank, and I know how much he meant what he said, and how much the words themselves mean."

To quote Ray Bolger: "The philosophy of *Oz* is man's search for basic human needs—a heart, brains, courage. And that, chum, will never be old hat."

Recently, Jack Haley, now retired, said, "There's nothing to date that picture. I get more fan requests for photographs now than I did when I was a star. I love the film because I wasn't anything to my six-year-old grandson, then he saw the film and now I'm a king!"

As Haley put it, "*The Wizard of Oz* is a toy for a new group of kids every year." They are transfixed before their sets by its colorful

story, in spite of—or maybe in the case of some macabre-minded youngsters, *because* of—the production's horrific elements: there is a nightmarish disorientation for some children about the prolonged efforts of a little-girl-lost to find her way home from a strange land, and then there are the more literal terrors like witches and Winged Monkeys. Adults can re-enter the fanciful world of childhood, as well as marvel at the movie's opulent know-how.

Some—perhaps moistly—recognize, too, that Dorothy's struggle to find happiness is analogous to the legendary Judy's.

On June 22, 1969, Judy Garland, emaciated and old-looking far beyond her forty-seven years, died while staying in London with her fifth husband, Mickey Deans, a discothèque manager she had married three months earlier.* The body was flown back to the United States, where her make-up man on *The Wizard of Oz* thirty years before, Charles Schram, again prepared her for a devoted public—for the last time. The coroner's verdict was that she had died accidentally from "an incautious self-overdosage" of sleeping pills; but Liza told newsmen, "I think Mama was just tired like a flower that blooms and gives joy to the world, then wilts away."

Most of the other prominent players in *Wizard* also have succumbed: Frank Morgan, in 1949; Charley Grapewin, 1956; Clara Blandick, 1962 (at eighty-one, by suicide!); Bert Lahr, 1967; and Billie Burke, 1970.

Haley recently had serious abdominal surgery, but Bolger and Miss Hamilton—both in their seventies—continue to work on stage, screen and television. Miss Hamilton is especially visible through her television commercials as Cora, the country storekeeper who sells only Maxwell House Coffee.

In May, 1970, MGM, fighting for survival in a changed industry, held a public auction of studio props and costumes on Stage 27 of the Culver City lot. Among the costumes, Bert

Lahr's Cowardly Lion rig went for $2,400, while a trenchcoat of Clark Gable's was picked up for $1,250 and Elizabeth Taylor's *Father of the Bride* (1950) wedding dress sold for $625. Even a somewhat gamy Tarzan (Johnny Weissmuller) loincloth drew $200.

The most prized items, though, were the ruby red slippers worn by Judy Garland in *The Wizard of Oz*. Before the bidding began, the Mayor of Culver City gave a speech in which he begged to be allowed to retain the slippers for public display in that city:

> In a world where even our little children look with awe and sometimes, I'm afraid, with favor on the use of narcotics and mind-expanding drugs as a means of adventure, you can understand how refreshing it is to have not just a few, but hundreds of letters and petitions, many of them written on notebook paper, asking me to try and save the one object that is the symbol of everything that is pure and clean in the world of make-believe. I am here tonight in a desperate attempt to plead with you to allow the children and citizens of Culver City to retain an item that was literally born here. We beg you not to bid against us for the ruby red slippers.

Spectators' sniffles were absorbed by thunderous applause, and the bidding began for the size 4½ slippers. The first bid was $1,000, five hundred more than the Mayor was able to offer. The final bid was for $15,000, from a lawyer representing a California millionaire who wished to remain anonymous. Afterward, confusion reigned briefly when a Memphis matron claimed she won the real shoes thirty years before in a national movie contest. Hers were size 6B, though, which were much larger than Judy wore; so it seemed the pair auctioned off by MGM had been the genuine articles.

Dorothy's/Judy's magic little red slippers had come to the end of the Yellow Brick Road.

*Judy's four other husbands: musician David Rose, 1941-43; director Vincente Minnelli, 1945-51; promoter Sid Luft, 1952-65; and actor Mark Herron, 1965-67.

THE WIZARD OF OZ

CREDITS

Metro-Goldwyn-Mayer Presents
A Victor Fleming Production

THE CAST

Dorothy. . . . . Judy Garland
Professor Marvel. . . . . Frank Morgan
Hunk . . . . Ray Bolger
Zeke . . . . Bert Lahr
Hickory . . . . Jack Haley
Glinda. . . . . Billie Burke
Miss Gulch . . . . Margaret Hamilton
Uncle Henry. . . . . Charley Grapewin
Nikko . . . . Pat Walshe
Auntie Em. . . . . Clara Blandick
Toto . . . . Toto

and The Munchkins

Directed by Victor Fleming
Produced by Mervyn LeRoy
Screenplay by
Noel Langley, Florence Ryerson and Edgar Allan Woolf
Adaptation by Noel Langley
From the book by L. Frank Baum
Musical Adaptation by Herbert Stothart
The Lyrics: E. Y. Harburg
The Music: Harold Arlen
Associate Conductor: George Stoll
Orchestral and Vocal Arrangements:
George Bassman, Murray Cutter,
Paul Marquardt and Ken Darby
Musical Numbers Staged by Bobby Connolly
Photographed in Technicolor by Harold Rosson, A.S.C.
Associate: Allen Davey, A.S.C.
Technicolor Color Director: Natalie Kalmus
Associate: Henri Jaffa
Recording Director: Douglas Shearer
Art Director: Cedric Gibbons
Associate: William A. Horning
Set Decorations by Edwin B. Willis
Special Effects by Arnold Gillespie
Costumes by Adrian
Character Make-ups Created by Jack Dawn
Film Editor: Blanche Sewell
Running Time: 100 minutes

BIBLIOGRAPHY

BOOKS

Deans, Mickey and Pinchot, Ann. *Weep No More, My Lady.* New York: Hawthorn, 1972.

DiOrio, Jr., Al. *Little Girl Lost.* New Rochelle, N.Y.: Arlington House, 1973.

Edwards, Anne. *Judy Garland.* New York: Simon and Schuster, 1975.

Fields, W. C. and Fields, Ronald J. *W. C. Fields by Himself.* New York: Warner Paperback Library, 1974.

Fordin, Hugh, *The World of Entertainment!* Garden City, N.Y.: Doubleday & Co., 1975.

Frank, Gerold. *Judy.* New York: Harper & Row, 1975.

Jablonski, Edward. *Harold Arlen: Happy with the Blues.* Garden City, N.Y.: Doubleday & Co., 1961.

Karr, Kathleen, editor. *The American Film Heritage.* Washington, D.C.: Acropolis Books, Ltd., 1972.

Lahr, John. *Notes on a Cowardly Lion.* New York: Alfred A. Knopf, 1969.

Lambert, Gavin. *GWTW: The Making of Gone with the Wind.* Boston: Little, Brown and Company, 1973.

LeRoy, Mervyn and Kleiner, Dick. *Take One.* New York: Hawthorn, 1974.

Minnelli, Vincente and Arce, Hector. *I Remember It Well.* Garden City, N.Y.: Doubleday & Co., 1974.

Morella, Joe and Epstein, Edward. *Judy: The Films and Career of Judy Garland.* New York: Citadel Press, Inc., 1969.

Parish, James Robert and Ano, Jack. *Liza!* New York: Pocket Books, 1975.

Parish, James Robert and Bowers, Ronald L. *The MGM Stock Company.* New Rochelle, N.Y.: Arlington House, 1973.

Rosenberg, Bernard and Silverstein, Harry. *The Real Tinsel.* New York: Macmillan Company, 1970.

Schickel, Richard. *The Men Who Made the Movies.* New York: Atheneum, 1975.

Sennett, Ted, editor. *The Movie Buff's Book.* New York: Pyramid, 1975.

Steen, Mike. *Hollywood Speaks.* New York: G. P. Putnam's Sons, 1974.

Thomas, Lawrence B. *The MGM Years.* New York: Columbia House, 1972.

Tormé, Mel. *The Other Side of the Rainbow: With Judy Garland on the Dawn Patrol.* New York: William Morrow and Company, 1970.

Wilk, Max. *They're Playing Our Song.* New York: Atheneum, 1973.

MAGAZINES and NEWSPAPERS

After Dark
Film Careers: Judy Garland
Film Fan Monthly
Films and Filming
Films in Review
Focus on Film
High Fidelity
The Hollywood Reporter
Liberty
The Newark Evening News

The New Republic
The New York Daily News
The New York Journal-American
The New York Post
The New York Times
The New York World-Telegram
Photoplay Studies
Time
TV Guide
Variety